EXPANDED PRACTICE
HÖWELER + YOON ARCHITECTU|

J. Meejin Yoon and Eric Höweler

Published by
Princeton Architectural Press
37 East Seventh Street
New York, New York 10003

For a free catalog of books, call 1 800 722 6657.
Visit our website at www.papress.com.

Photo and image credits:
David Heald, courtesy of the Solomon R. Guggenheim Foundation:
24, 26, 28 middle, 29
Alan Karchmer: 145, 174 bottom
Andy Ryan: 164, 165
Franco Vairani, Squared Design Lab: 99, 101, 102, 104, 105, 179, 183

HYA/MYS would like to thank Jennifer Chuong, Katie Flynn, Deborah
Grossberg, Saran Oki, Lisa Pauli, Ryan Pinkham, Joe Michael, Ryan Murphy,
Shani Cho, and Buck Sleeper for their contributions to this book.

Editor: Becca Casbon
Designer: Omnivore

Special thanks to: Nettie Aljian, Bree Anne Apperley, Sara Bader, Nicola
Bednarek, Janet Behning, Carina Cha, Penny (Yuen Pik) Chu, Carolyn
Deuschle, Russell Fernandez, Pete Fitzpatrick, Wendy Fuller, Jan Haux,
Clare Jacobson, Aileen Kwun, Nancy Eklund Later, Linda Lee, Laurie Manfra,
John Myers, Katharine Myers, Lauren Nelson Packard, Dan Simon, Andrew
Stepanian, Jennifer Thompson, Paul Wagner, Joseph Weston, and Deb Wood
of Princeton Architectural Press
—Kevin C. Lippert, publisher

Library of Congress Cataloging-in-Publication Data
Yoon, J. Meejin (Jeannie Meejin), 1972-
 Expanded practice : Höweler + Yoon Architecture/My Studio / J. Meejin Yoon
and Eric Höweler. — 1st ed.
   p. cm.
ISBN 978-1-56898-866-5 (alk. paper)
1. Höweler + Yoon Architecture/My Studio. 2. Architecture—United
States—History—21st century. 3. Design—United States—History—
21st century. I. Höweler, Eric, 1972- II. Title. III. Title: Höweler + Yoon
Architecture/My Studio.
NA737.H69A4 2009
724'.7—dc22
                    2008048440

CONTENTS

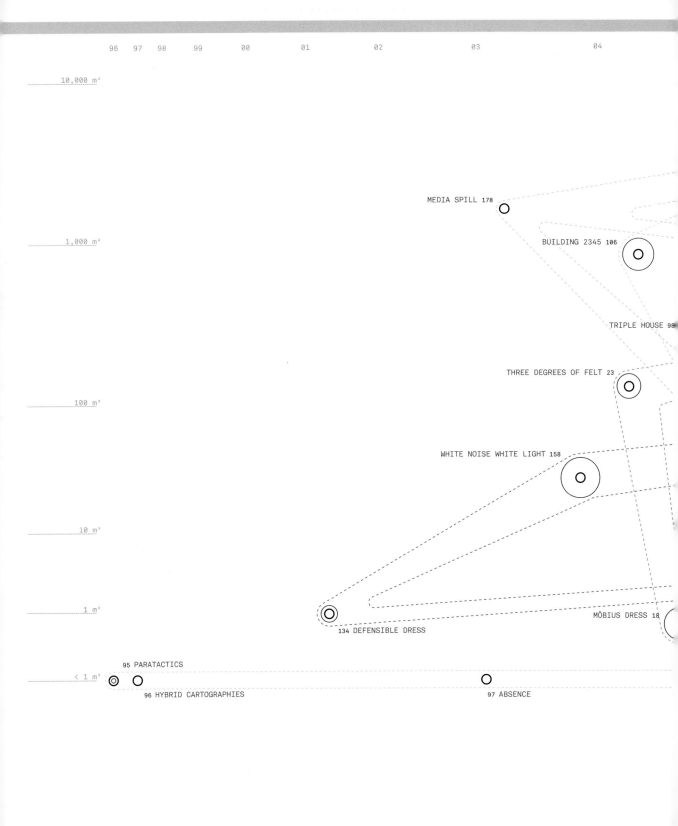

96 97 98 99   00   01   02   03   04

10,000 m²

1,000 m²

MEDIA SPILL 178

BUILDING 2345 106

TRIPLE HOUSE 98

THREE DEGREES OF FELT 23

100 m²

WHITE NOISE WHITE LIGHT 158

10 m²

1 m²

MÖBIUS DRESS 18

134 DEFENSIBLE DRESS

95 PARATACTICS

< 1 m²

96 HYBRID CARTOGRAPHIES   97 ABSENCE

05   06   07   08

118 NET-X-INGS

184 MEADOWLANDS

188
PUBLIC WORKS

120
SKY COURTS

112 HAYDEN SRO

44 HOTEL ΔT

81 BRIDGE HOUSE

175 WHITE HOUSE WHITE SCREEN

150 HOVER

TRIO 41

65 OUTSIDE IN LOFT

73 CLIFF STREET HOUSE

144 HI FI

31 PS1 LOOP

62 PIXEL FIELD

170 LOW REZ

139 ENTASIS

39 LOOP CHAIRS

94 TRAVEL REPORTS

ANATOMY OF A DOT

The diagrams introducing each chapter serve as composite
mappings of projects, linkages, and research streams. Each
project is located by a dot whose size is dependent on the
number of conceptual links it shares with other projects.
The dot's location within the diagram is determined by
chronology (the horizontal axis) and scale (the vertical
axis). The resulting webs illustrate the proliferation of
shared preoccupations, cross-pollination, and feedback
loops within the larger matrix.

EXPANDED PRACTICE
J. Meejin Yoon and Eric Höweler

CASCADE

On April 27, 1986, at 7:00 AM, a nuclear engineer set off an alarm as he arrived at the Forsmark nuclear power plant in Sweden. High levels of radiation were discovered on the soles of his shoes. As Forsmark officials instigated emergency protocols, authorities were notified of possible nuclear fallout, inciting a national panic. Within hours, radioactive coatings on the ground were detected in Sweden's Oskarshamn, Barsebäck, and Ringhals nuclear power plants. However, after extensive testing, it was determined that the radioactive matter had not originated at Forsmark, or at any other Nordic nuclear power plant.

Over twenty-nine hours earlier, reactor number four at the Chernobyl plant in the Ukrainian SSR had exploded, causing a chain of other explosions and sending highly radioactive fallout into the atmosphere. Carried by winds, the radioactive particles drifted over the western Soviet Union, eastern and northern Europe, and as far as the east coast of North America. It was Sweden's search for the source of radioactivity that led to the discovery of this serious nuclear disaster, seven hundred miles away in the western Soviet Union. After officials in Sweden raised worldwide alarm, the Kremlin eventually admitted that the accident had occurred.

The disaster was a watershed moment—an ecological crisis that spread beyond political and geographical borders with a truly global cascade of effects. The reactor meltdown, the weather patterns, and the scientist's shoe were bound together in a network of causes and effects. In the wake of the disaster, an ecological consciousness emerged that underscored the interconnectedness of all things; actions are relational, nature is contingent, and effects are measurable.

NETWORK

As we become increasingly aware of the interdependence of our collective ecological footprints, we also become increasingly connected through network structures of communication and information exchange. The network—a horizontal and distributed organizational model—is the contemporary organizational paradigm, impacting all cultural and technological modes of production. It blankets the globe, linking nodes, places, and individuals. It has produced a pervasive "climate" of connectivity.

The coverage of information networks has created a new "ecology of technologies" in which relationships between people and places are mediated by the ubiquity of the network. This condition of networked culture has affected every aspect of politics, economics, and culture. It has reordered historical hierarchies of center and periphery, high and low, expertise and opinion. Bottom-up movements have utilized the internet to create communities of interests, challenging centralized information structures. The structures of communication have also spawned a deluge of content; spam, feeds, and email have created a new state of distractedness and a new attention economy.

These two cultural conditions—the consciousness of ecological interdependence and the ubiquity of network culture—mark the contemporary moment as distinct from the recent past. New modes of action, forms of production, and types of agency have been radicalized by the emerging currency of access. Reorganizing the way we see the world and the way we operate within it, this paradigm shift has affected a generation of cultural producers, creating new "ecologies of practice" and new modes of architectural production. Ecology is defined as the study of relationships and interactions between organisms and their environments; in the emerging ecologies of practice, relationships between cultural producers are reconfigured, extended, and amplified by new technologies.

CONTEMPORARY

Unlike the zeitgeist, understood as an inescapable and pervasive cultural condition, the contemporary is more explicit, specific, and instrumental. While the zeitgeist is simply "in the air"—like the radioactive cloud—the contemporary must be actively constructed. It is not natural or by default; rather it is willed, authored, and actively taken up in response to the conditions of its time. Architecture, while striving to be timeless, must also be timely. Contemporaneity in architecture requires self-consciousness of the broader field of cultural production, as well as an active agenda for the engagement of that expanded field. The contemporary is by design.

EXPANDED

Höweler + Yoon Architecture / MY Studio is part of a new generation of architects that see the contemporary as their Project. At once critical of its construction and celebratory of its potential, we grapple with both the sober and the capricious aspects of the contemporary. We are conscious of the misalignments between the significant social, political, and environmental changes of our time and the internal debates and preoccupations of our own discipline. In order to be relevant, architecture must address the contemporary, and it is within this unfolding context that we have found it imperative to engage architecture in an expanded field, or as an Expanded Practice—a practice grounded in the discipline of architecture but not limited by its boundaries. In physics, thermal expansion is the tendency of matter to change in volume as a response to a change in temperature. As architects, embedded in the conceptual and physical production of the contemporary condition, we are acutely aware of the "changing temperature of the age."

The scope of an Expanded Practice is necessarily both broad and specific. Its research agendas take into account a wide range of sources, causes, and effects, looking at phenomena forensically at multiple scales and across different disciplinary territories. Echoing the entangled complicity of the communications network, the radioactive cloud, and the scientist's shoe, the scope of this practice is necessarily multiple. As architects, situated against the backdrop of accelerating ecological, informational, technological, and cultural connectedness, we see ourselves as participants in the production of this interconnected environment.

DISCIPLINARITY

The discipline of architecture has been delimited simultaneously on two fronts. Traditional notions of a bounded architectural practice are the result of a regulating professionalism, which has defined the body of knowledge that is constitutive of the discipline of architecture. This jurisdictional delimiting of expertise seeks to ensure public health, safety, and welfare, and regulates the extents of the profession. Within the tradition of academic architectural practices, a "critical practice" has defined an equally insular project of "autonomy," where architecture investigates issues specific to its own discipline, segregated from extra-disciplinary concerns of the practice, the market, and the public. The Expanded Practice aims to broaden the definition of architecture, uncovering new productive territories within an expansive disciplinary network. This definition includes a wider range of "rights and responsibilities," including the roles of protagonist in the production of the built environment and articulator of the larger cultural conditions that affect it.

APPLIED

In our Expanded Practice, design is engaged as a form of applied research. Its techniques and methods ensure that knowledge produced is accumulated, pooled, and redeployed. Echoing the research framework proposed by Stanford Anderson in which the resonance among parallel research programs enriches and grants each greater credibility, our practice embraces multiple simultaneous streams of research. We have identified five parallel research streams in this book—ENVELOPES, NATURES, FORMATS, INTERACTIONS, and MEDIA—each integrally connected to our understanding of the contemporary and its built environment. Seeking to embrace "the productive tension between theory and experiment… between abstract knowledge and practice,"[1] we foster within each of these streams both conceptual and artifactual agendas, continuously moving back and forth between them. Each project is an opportunity to test concepts at various scales. It is through the intersections, cross-pollinations, and feedbacks within each stream and across streams that we achieve an Expanded Practice.

STREAMS

Beginning with the body, ENVELOPES looks at a series of projects that deploy surface techniques and strategies to extend the body in space. Technological advances have projected the scientific gaze into the macroscale of the universe and the microscale of the atom. The body, with its interior territories and functions, constitutes an internal horizon whose status is still an essential object of inquiry. Even as technologies allow for new virtual bodies and synthetic body parts, the body itself is still a primary instrument and sensorial device. Envelopes extend the body outward, from the garment to the building to the landscape. By investigating the limits and extensions of the body, we seek to expand our understanding of the architectural skin as a formal, organizational, and perceptual interface between the human body and the built environment.

NATURES gathers a group of projects that engage the status of "the natural" within the built environment. The legacy of human action on the environment has ensured that all sites are in some way marked by human presence. The "new" natural is understood as always already contaminated by human action. Given this post-pastoral context, the natural is contingent on its relationship to the artificial. The term "nature" is also related to the status of the natural and familiar: the normative, comfortable, and domesticated. Domestic architectures often strive to "naturalize" a given context in the construction of the familiar. The strategy of defamiliarization is deployed in several projects within the chapter to reconfigure normative relationships between figure and ground, inside and outside, vertical and horizontal, in order to challenge our assumptions concerning architecture's role in the production of the "natural."

The proliferation and influence of new horizontal and nonhierarchical structures necessitates an examination of accepted organizational systems within architecture. By reexamining the role of ordering strategies, projects in the FORMATS section investigate the use of frameworks, rules, and parameters as a starting point of design. Each of the projects in this chapter dissects formats ranging from print and publication structures to zoning regulations and architecture typologies. By carefully examining rules, constraints, and assumptions, new possibilities both formal and informal emerge from the rules themselves. These projects confront organizational and regulatory logics as part of design research and seek unconventional configurations borne out of their limits.

The ubiquity of computing has created an "open source" culture where information is increasingly accessible and technology is naturalized. Our physical environment has become saturated with information displays, interactive interfaces, and sensing devices. While, arguably, architecture has always been responsive, encouraging interaction between a space and the people that use it, new technological developments are putting pressure on architecture to become more adaptable and intelligent. Technology has become increasingly customizable—such devices as the microcontroller, infrared sensor, and radio-frequency identification (RFID) tag enable a tighter integration between architecture and electronics, hardware, and software. The projects in the INTERACTIONS section incorporate responsive technologies to create an "open work" which relies on the interaction of an outside stimulus (a foreign body) to complete it. Often situated within public space, these techno-architectural interventions become mediating devices between the users and the site. The body and the relationships between bodies are repositioned through these sensorial environments. It is through the actions of the public that these projects transform from merely responsive to adaptive.

MEDIA explores increasingly intertwined sets of relationships between producers (content creators), consumers (content receivers), and their interfaces (mediating devices) within a structure of communication where architecture is implicated. While the Gothic cathedral was an early form of architectural broadcast, with the content inscribed in stone, contemporary architecture has evolved to accommodate electronic broadcast technologies and is today reconfigured by the port and the terminal to become an interface itself. The projects in the MEDIA section investigate the role of architecture as a mediating mechanism, or conduit, within the broader cultural phenomena of broadcast and spectacle. They recast architecture as a mass medium capable of producing a new public that engages the structures of communication and transmission, transforming the viewer from a passive recipient into an active agent.

STRUCTURE

The diagrams introducing each chapter serve as composite mappings of projects, linkages, and research streams, laid out horizontally by time and vertically by scale. Each individual project is located by an icon whose dilation responds to the number of linkages the project has to other projects inside and outside its research stream. The resulting webs of research agendas illustrate the degree of cross-pollination, linkages, and feedback loops within the larger matrix of projects. The linkages across research streams highlight secondary or informal relationships. Reading the alternate orders within the matrix reveals shared preoccupations across streams. These cross platforms examine the new relationships between form and performance as well as those between technologies, tactics, and techniques.

ALL

The microscopic particles detected on the shoes worn by the Swedish nuclear engineer were the first indicator of the nuclear disaster that was unfolding seven hundred miles away. The shoe became the site, the index, and the signal, while the meteorological conditions that dispersed the radioactive particles were the distribution mechanism. The interaction between the two led to a heightened understanding of the relationships between human actions and environmental effects. The ecologies of contamination, communication, action, and effect are all fundamentally about interaction. The scope of an Expanded Practice takes on these reconfigured ecologies of the built environment to engage the critical issues of our time. In our work, we investigate causes and effects, exploring issues that arise out of specific conditions of the contemporary, related to the body, technology, public space, human experience, and the built environment. These projects, whether installations, armatures, furniture, or buildings, are all architectures in the fullest sense of the word—they engage a material and spatial practice that is constructed, experienced, and perceived. This Expanded Practice is necessarily multiple and specific, working at the scale of the shoe, the network, and the cloud.

1. Stanford Anderson, "Architectural Design as a Series of Research Programs," in Architectural Theory Since 1968, ed. K. Michael Hays (Cambridge, MA: MIT Press, 2000), 490–505.

REIMAGINING PROPINQUITY: THE WORK OF HÖWELER + YOON ARCHITECTURE / MY STUDIO

Andrew Payne and Rodolphe el-Khoury

The work of Höweler + Yoon Architecture / MY Studio (here-after HYA/MYS) is animated by a set of dedications and preoccupations familiar from contemporary discussions of architecture. Their pursuit of the new plastic freedom afforded by the digitalization of the design process, their interest in the sensorial potentials opened up by the architectural deployment of intelligent surfaces, their preference for an atmospheric aesthetic organized around transitive phenomena, their understanding of architecture as working between the materiality of built form and the immateriality of the informational networks that traverse and inhabit it, their commitment to seek-ing out new reciprocities between artificial and living systems—all are in sympathy with a broadly shared con-ception of what the issues and opportunities facing the discipline today are. Similarly representative is their ambition to negotiate between professional realism and a view of architecture as a research practice that has affinities with both the experimental ambitions of the twentieth century avant-gardes and the more ideologically circumspect trajectories of ecological, technological, and social/cultural investigation that today constellate under the rubric of product design semantics.[1] What per-haps distinguishes the work of HYA/MYS from that of many of their contemporaries is the way in which these com-mitments are focused around a sustained attention to the role that built form has in shaping the experience of propinquity at the three scales that have stratified the architectural imagination since Vitruvius: that of the body, that of the building, that of the city. The experience of "being-with" as it unfolds at these three scales is the special concern of their research, and the enigmatic object of the experiments to which that research gives rise. In what follows, we will briefly discuss three projects that we imagine to be respectively representative of these three scales: the Defensible Dress, PS1 Loop, and White Noise White Light. First, however, a few words about the quality and substance of that propinquity that is the central stake of this work.

In order to both distinguish the sense of propinquity that is at work in these projects and to appreciate its contemporaneity, it is perhaps useful to briefly compare it to the conception of propinquity that was at play in the theorizations of "public space" employed by postmodern theorists of the urban condition like George Baird, Kenneth Frampton, and Richard Sennett. The conception of propinquity that is developed in different ways by these three theorists is aptly summarized in Hannah Arendt's description of the Greek agora—her model public sphere—as a space of reciprocal appearance, a space of dialogue, and a space of plural and co-implicated agency. According to Baird, Frampton, and Sennett, the forms of collective appearance, speech, and action that were invented in ancient Athens as well as the built world connate with those forms are today threatened by the forces of capitalization and the erosion of the democratic political traditions that these forces have instigated. In response to that erosion, Baird, Frampton, and Sennett call for both a reinvigoration of the forms of embodied appearance, speech, and action that have traditionally defined public life in the West and a reinvention of the architectural idioms designed to accommodate that life. By contrast, the conception of propinquity advanced by HYA/MYS, as by many of their contemporaries, is one in which the distinction between public and private modalities of social experience, so central to the conception of propinquity advanced by Arendt and her architectural avatars, gives way to an at once more pervasive and less determinate experience of "being-with," an experience of original and insuperable self-differing as much constitutive of individual as collective experience, and therefore operative at all scales and in all modalities of occupation.

The collective experience to which HYA/MYS direct their attention is one in which the carnal copresence of political agents so dear to the Arendtian conception of propinquity is vitiated by a plethora of communicative technologies designed to mediate, simulate, and increasingly, to supplant it. The collective experience to which they direct their attention is also one in which the forms of critical reflection and responsible self-disclosure that the Arendtian conception of speech suggests give way to the instrumental and largely anonymous modalities of communication associated with contemporary information culture. Finally, the collective experience to which they direct their attention is one in which the Arendtian emphasis on action is inflected by, on the one hand, a renewed interest in the role that our perceptual and affective faculties have in the construction of collective experience, and, on the other, an emphasis on the ludic or theatrical, as against the instrumental or practical implications of the verb "to act." It is from the perspective of this transformed conception of the space of appearance and the forms of discourse and action that such a space affords that HYA/MYS's work at all scales must be understood. With these summary comments in mind, let us turn to the three projects mentioned previously, in order to better appreciate how they respond to this transformed sense of collective experience and architecture's role in shaping it.

DEFENSIBLE DRESS
In recent history, a lively exchange has transpired between clothing designers and architects. As more than one commentator has observed, this exchange has deep roots in the analogy between building and raiment that shaped the theory and practice of late-nineteenth-century and early-twentieth-century architecture. As in the first instance, the current pursuit of this analogy is organized not merely around shared structural and aesthetic concerns, but also around a shared curiosity about how individuals and communities of individuals negotiate the new modes of propinquity arising from new forms of metropolitanization.

One expression of the current intersection of clothing design and architecture is the emergence of a new order of urban artifact that is situated ambiguously between the status of a garment and a building, often with intelligent technologies of one sort or another serving as the mediator between these distinct artifactual realms. Thinking from the side of clothing, Hussein Chalayan's Remote Control Dress—which integrates wireless technology, electrical circuitry, and automated commands after a fashion that recalls the intelligent architectures of our day—is in many respects exemplary of this new confluence of garment and building design. In a slightly different vein, Lucy Orta's various experiments in intimate architecture, the scale and structure of which suggest a complex of at once minimal and nomadic dwellings, are noteworthy for the way that they link communities of wearers by clothing them in a single collective garment that prescribes novel ratiocinations of collective organization and individual autonomy. Thinking from the side of architecture, the role played by the "braincoat" in Diller + Scofidio's original proposal for their Blur Building is exemplary of the way in which architects are also engaging the full spectrum of membrane structures, shaping our relationship to our surroundings in an effort to question and reorder the terms of contemporary social engagement.

HYA/MYS's Defensible Dress (2001) is an artifact entirely in this vein. Incorporating sensory technologies, a circuit board, and a series of actuated quills, the dress allows its wearer to program a microcontroller that, by sending an electronic current through Flexinol ligaments embedded in each of the quills, operates the ligament like a lever, thereby prompting a horizontal extension of the quills, and with that extension an aggressive expansion of the wearer's space of embodied occupation. We might say that the extension of the quills translates the ethical and social imperative to exercise tact in or dealings with others (noli me tangere) into an implacable fact. As in the work of other artists and architects exploring the uncanny and at times even sinister underside of intelligent machines—the sculptural installations of Philip Beesley come immediately to mind—the Defensible Dress gives positive figure to unresolved ambiguities, tensions, and resistances arising from the current technological transformation of our socius. By concretizing the garment's charismatic aura, giving it literal form and material extent, the Defensible Dress underlines the contested nature of even the most intimate experiences of propinquity.

Another garment project, the Möbius Dress, represents a kindred material meditation on the negotiable thresholds that comprise intersubjective experience in the contemporary setting. Challenging "clothing's absolute adherence to conventions of interiority and exteriority" (Yoon), the Möbius Dress represents a kind of sartorial synecdoche of Jean-Luc Nancy's reconception of the social bond as a (k)not to be incessantly untied and retied: "The (k)not [of being-with] involves neither interiority nor exteriority, but…in being tied, ceaselessly makes the inside pass outside, each into (or by way of) the other, the other inside, turning endlessly back on itself without returning to itself…the tying of the (k)not is nothing but the putting into relation that presupposes at once proximity and distance, attachment and detachment, intricacy, intrigue and ambivalence."[2]

PS1 LOOP

A similar ambiguity is sustained in PS1 Loop. In this work, HYA/MYS distill the salient ideas of their practice in an installation proposal for the 2006 MoMA/PS1 Young Architects Program. Installation projects, especially as framed by this program, constitute an R&D genre for emerging practices, and have repeatedly offered HYA/MYS opportunities for aligning professional and practical interests with an experimental agenda.

Tightly filling its site with a continuous polypropylene ribbon, PS1 Loop explores Voronoi packing geometry to build an intricately variegated three-dimensional matrix in the museum's courtyard. The ribbon performs as both support and enclosure, continuously folding and twisting to densely occupy the courtyard with a variety of cellular configurations. Differing in size, orientation, and position, the local surfaces produced by the ribbon's continuous extension suggest a variety of familiar functions (table, bench, et cetera), while at the same time remaining available for unprescribed forms of occupation and appropriation.

The installation is a tour de force of manufacturing and building innovation, aligning cutting-edge experimentation in geometry with new materials and fabrication methods. This line of research into packing and minimal surface geometry has already produced interesting buildings, such PTW Architects' Watercube for the Beijing Olympics, and promises more important results in optimizing structure and reducing building mass in the pressing quest for lightness in architecture. HYA/MYS add a twist to such experiments with irregular geometry and structure by conflating surface and vector active components, building the entire structure with eighteen-inch-wide plastic sheets.

The technique brings to mind experiments by Office dA such as Voromuro and Voroduo, where the material, structural, and surface qualities of thin polycarbonate strips are exploited in most ingenious and unexpected geometrical iterations. However, while Office dA's intricately convoluted ribbons are deployed in configurations we still recognize in conventional architectural terms (wall, roof, dome) and clearly demarcate enclosure, HYA/MYS's plastic loops transgress the defining limits—physical and conceptual—between space and enclosure to occupy the entire space with a foamlike architecture. At once volumetric and planar, full and empty, massive in its consistent and homogeneous materiality and ultrafine in its constituent parts, this built foam subverts familiar distinctions between wall and space, solid and void. To enter PS1 Loop is to become enmeshed in a latticework of pliant surfaces that promote a sense of collective occupation as dependent on our affective responses as on our intellectual responses.

WHITE NOISE WHITE LIGHT

The preoccupations that we have observed to be at play in the work of HYA/MYS at the scale of the body and the building are also apparent in their urban-scale interventions. These interventions often consist of temporary pavilions or event structures of one sort or another. Whether ephemeral or permanent, they invariably take the sensate body and its spatiotemporal envelope as the intimate locus of social connection. Having said that, this sensate body is treated as a body not merely susceptible to, but entirely traversed by and suffused with the informational networks that define contemporary social life. The White Noise White Light project that HYA/MYS installed for the 2004 Athens Olympics is a case in point. Situated on the public plaza facing that most auspicious of sites in the history of urban spectacle, the Theater of Dionysius, White Noise White Light transformed the plaza into a visitor-activated synaesthetic "sound- and light-scape" fed by a constellation of fiber-optic strands, infrared sensors, and outdoor

speakers. Movement of a visitor across the site would prompt the fiber-optic outlets to transmit light from white LEDs, while at the same time causing speakers situated below the installation's raised deck to emit Johnson Noise, a form of white noise produced from the thermal motions of electrons in a resistor carrying a current across an electronic circuit. The result of these transmissions was that each visitor's traversal of the site carried with it a spectral echo and afterglow, a physical and immediately collective memory that, after a fashion reminiscent of the Defensible Dress, amplified the visitor's charismatic aura so as to expand his or her sphere of social influence. At the same time, the project gave positive figure to the otherwise invisible complex of movements that comprise the site's collective psychogeography.

REIMAGINING PROPINQUITY

The interest of HYA/MYS's work lies not only in its timely exploration of a set of themes that currently holds the attention of the profession, but also in the persuasive way in which these themes (and the techniques, tactics, and stratagems they imply) are brought into communication with the more ethically and politically motivated dedications of the generation that preceded them. At once insisting on propinquity as the fundamental condition to which architecture is in response, and demanding that, in thinking about and responding to this condition, we give sober consideration to the massively changed circumstances under which we continue to differ together, HYA/MYS present a model of how professional circumspection and social commitment, technical adroitness and critical reflection, robust construction and sensitivity to phenomenological effects can coexist to produce an architecture in which aesthetic experience rediscovers its social context and reinvents its political vocation.

1. Klaus Krippendorff, "On the Essential Contexts of Artifacts or on the Proposition that 'Design is Making Sense (of Things),'" The Idea of Design: A Design Issues Reader, ed. Victor Margolin and Richard Buchanan (Cambridge, MA: MIT Press, 1995), 57. Krippendorff describes product semantics, a variant of the term design semantics, as "a study of the symbolic qualities of man-made forms in the cognitive and social context of their use and the application of the knowledge gained to objects of industrial design."
2. Jean-Luc Nancy, The Sense of the World, trans. Jeffrey S. Librett (Minneapolis and London: University of Minnesota Press, 1997), 111.

RODOLPHE EL-KHOURY is Canada Research Chair in Architecture and Urban Design at the University of Toronto and partner in the design firm Khoury Levit Fong. He is the author of and contributor to numerous critically acclaimed books in architectural history and theory—including Monolithic Architecture, Architecture: In Fashion, Shaping the City: Studies in History, Theory and Urban Design, and See Through Ledoux: Architecture, Theatre, and the Pursuit of Transparency—and a regular contributor to professional and academic journals. He has received several awards and international recognition for his design work at Office dA, ReK Productions, and currently at KLF.

ANDREW PAYNE is a senior lecturer in the Daniels Faculty of Architecture, Landscape, and Design at the University of Toronto. He is currently working on two book manuscripts: Thales or Some Other: The Intellectual and Cultural Legacies of Construction, and Clamors of Being: the Genesis of Sense in Gilles Deleuze, Alain Badiou, Jacques Derrida, and Jean-Luc Nancy.

ENVELOPES

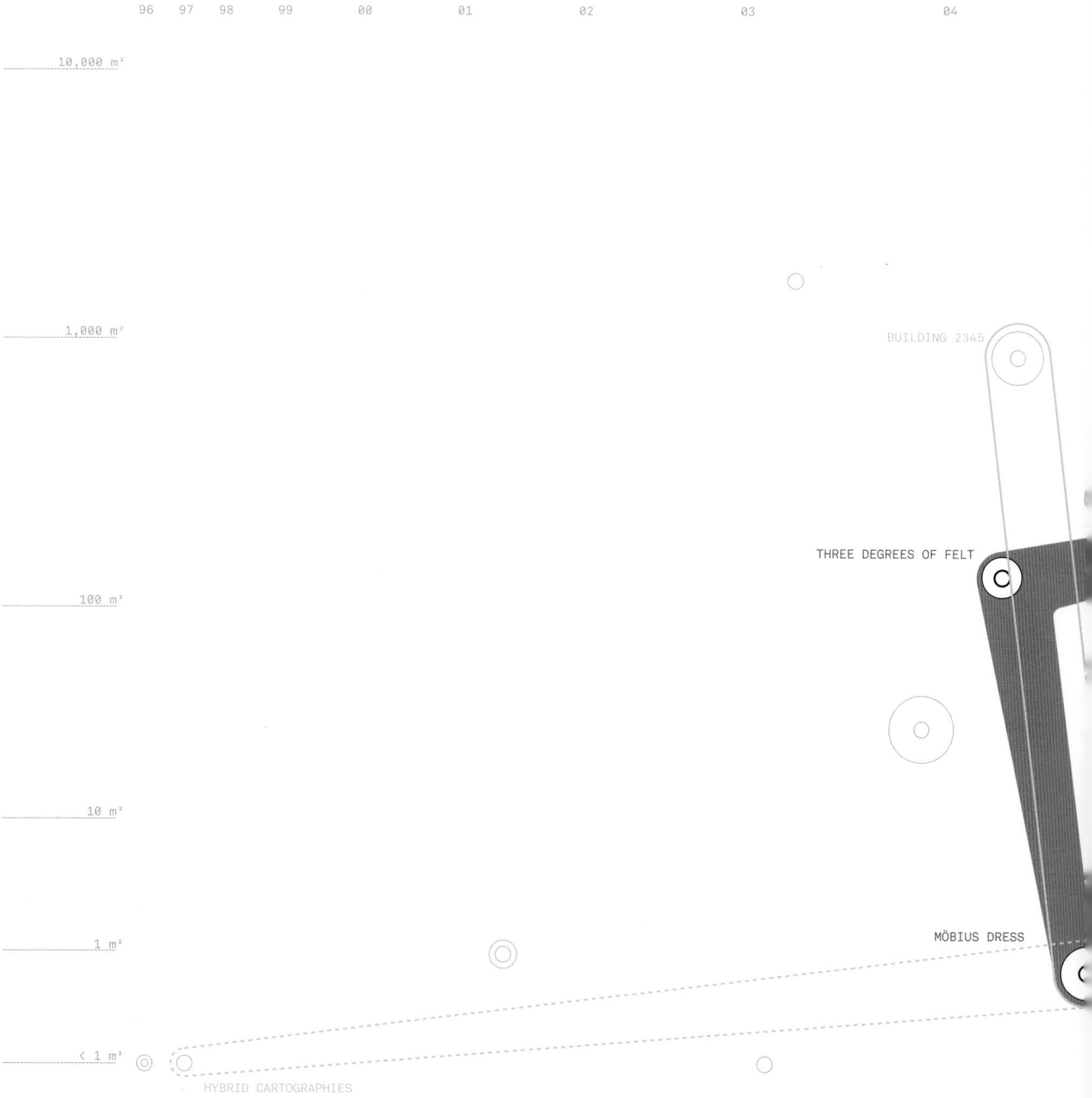

96 97 98   99   00   01   02   03   04

10,000 m²

1,000 m²

BUILDING 2345

THREE DEGREES OF FELT

100 m²

10 m²

1 m²

MÖBIUS DRESS

< 1 m²

HYBRID CARTOGRAPHIES

05   06   07   08

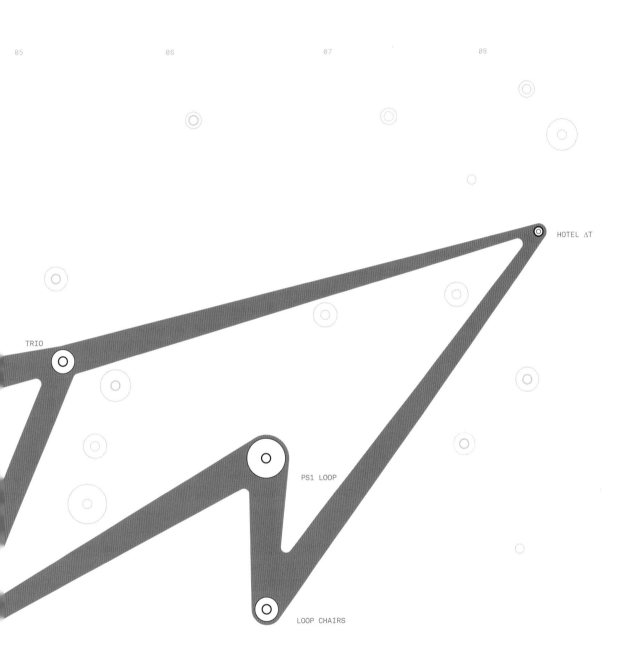

HOTEL ∆T

TRIO

PS1 LOOP

LOOP CHAIRS

Skin, the body's most immediate envelope and largest organ, is also its most sophisticated container. Protecting, insulating, regulating, absorbing, healing, and sensing, skin exemplifies the performative potential of a membrane envelope. Moving from one's body concentrically outwards, layers of membranes perform a spectrum of functions. From the scale of clothing to the scale of buildings, each of these constitutive skins differentiates and defines space, regulates temperature and moisture, and constructs internal and external relationships. In doing so, they also create interstitial conditions which negotiate function and sensation. In fact, each envelope is itself a spatial system, a complex and layered structure negotiating varying states—every envelope is an organ.

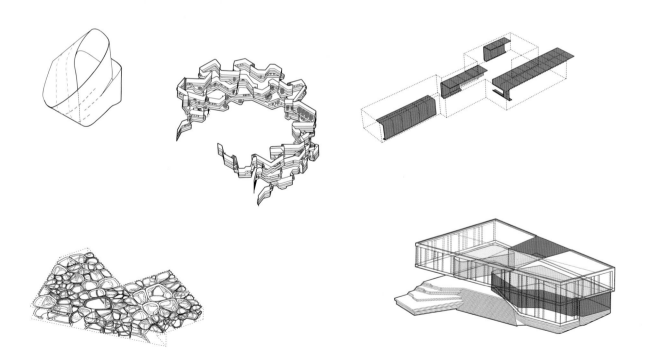

Locating the origins of architecture in a textile-based domestic tradition, Gottfried Semper makes clear connections between the cladding of a body and the cladding of a building. This etymological tracing, as paraphrased by Mary McLeod, links the German word "wand" (wall, partition, screen) to "gewand" (dress, garments, clothing) and the term "bekleidung" (dressing or cladding) to "kleidung" (clothing).[1] Affinities between fashion and architecture include a shared interest in the human body and the definition of space. Both disciplines engage the layered mediation between a body and its environment and the construction of social, political, and cultural identities.

Contemporary architectural practice shares techniques of surface manipulation with the tailor and dressmaker. The dressmaking pattern is a construction document, a two-dimensional document conveying intricate notational information for producing one or more three-dimensional constructs. Architects employ techniques including slitting, folding, pleating, and lining to manipulate and transform surface. This sharing of technique underscores not only embedded similarities between these disciplines and their conventions, but also an underlying desire to transform surfaces into productive, multifunctional membranes.

This intense interest in surface geometries has been an architectural preoccupation since the 1990s, when computer software and Deleuzian theory combined to produce topological architecture. More than a decade later, single-surface logics of contemporary form making—in which continuous folded surfaces supplant the differentiation of wall, floor, and ceiling—have been tested at a number of scales and with a variety of materials. Despite the exhaustive body of work exploring formal and tectonic potentials of surface, the performative potential of surface as a spatial construct continues to invite investigation.

This section of design research examines the relationship between the body and its wrappers, exploring how architectural surfaces can define an enclosure while maintaining a tangible or proximal connection to the body. The following projects investigate surface logics between the body and the environment, exploring the envelope as garment, furniture, structure, building, and landscape. The MÖBIUS DRESS applies the mathematical principle of a continuous loop to a material garment that confounds notions of interiority and exteriority. THREE DEGREES OF FELT, the exhibition design for the Aztec Empire show at the Solomon R. Guggenheim Museum, deploys a continuous folded envelope to house each of the exhibition's 400 artifacts, transforming surface into display infrastructure. PS1 LOOP proposes a continuous and structurally interdependent looped surface to create an inhabitable, immersive landscape. Similarly, a wrapper element in the TRIO lobby serves as a programmatic armature to accommodate seating, lighting, mailboxes, desk space, and entrance canopy. HOTEL ΔT examines multiple layers of envelope between the body and the environment. Wrapping from the body outward to modulate temperature and define the different wet and dry programs of the hotel and spa, the layers create varying conditioned zones and highlight the role of performance in the design process.

A shift in emphasis from what architecture looks like (form) and what architecture means (signification) to what architecture does (or how it performs)—culturally, materially, spatially, and environmentally—reflects a realignment of the influences of ecology and technology on architecture. This recalibration of form through performance updates the modernist mantra of form following function in response to the contemporary interconnectedness of architecture, technology, and ecology. The newly inscribed function of building envelopes makes Semper's textile-based reading of architecture newly salient; refocused on its intimate, bodily origins, the architectural envelope participates more precisely in performative, as well as formal, roles.

1. Mary McLeod, "Undressing Architecture: Fashion, Gender, and Modernity," in Architecture: In Fashion, ed. Deborah Fausch, Paulette Singley, Rodolphe el-Khoury, and Zvi Efrat (New York: Princeton Architectural Press, 1994), 48–49.

KNOT A LOOP

In examining the body and its material envelopes—skin, clothing, and architecture—the relationship between surface and space comes into question as a conceptual and corporeal construct. The MÖBIUS DRESS uses the mathematical principle of the möbius strip to reexamine surface as a seamless transformative condition between interior and exterior.

Through a simple splitting operation, cutting parallel to a strip's edges, the topological principles of the dress become visible as well as occupiable as the surface is divided into two intertwining loops. These loops conform to the body at different scales, meeting around the hips and torso. Operable zippers along the cut lines enable a continuous manipulation of surface, resulting in the dress's constantly evolving relationship to the body. The intact topology and changing form of the dress demonstrate a negotiation between the internal logics of a two-dimensional compact manifold and the external parameters of a three-dimensional structuring body.

The MÖBIUS DRESS is made from industrial recycled felt, a material created through friction as opposed to knitting or weaving. Homogenous, seamless, and grainless, felt is entirely nonorientable, exhibiting no difference between front and back and, when configured into a Möbius strip, no boundary between interior and exterior.

Applying a simple set of rules to an inherently supple geometry, the project challenges the conventional understanding of envelope as a delimiting condition. MÖBIUS DRESS provokes a rethinking of the assumed stable limits between interior and exterior, suggesting instead a smooth gradient between the two.

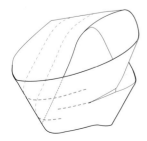

The Möbius strip is a one-sided, single-edged, nonorientable surface. The topological principles of the MÖBIUS DRESS enable it to perform as both envelope and spatial device.

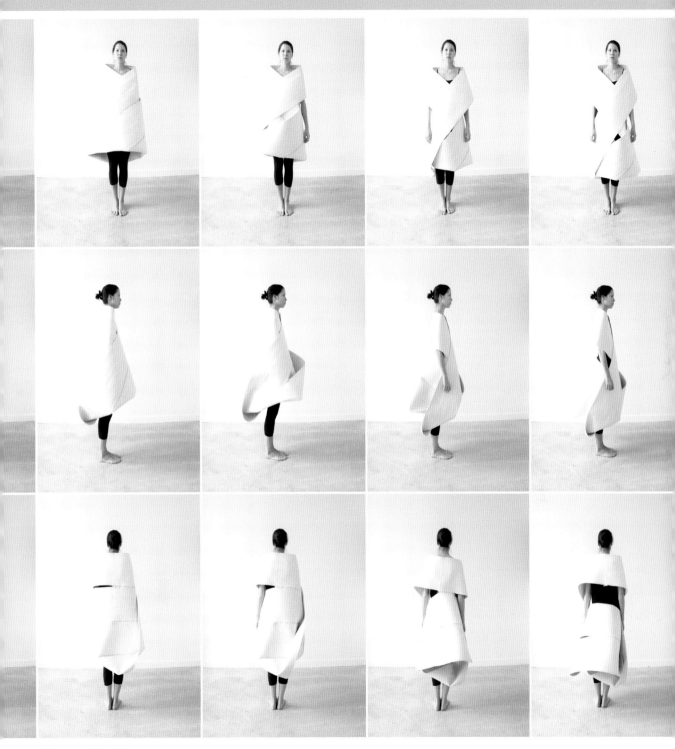

The form of the dress
as it unravels becomes
differentiated while
the surface remains
continuous.

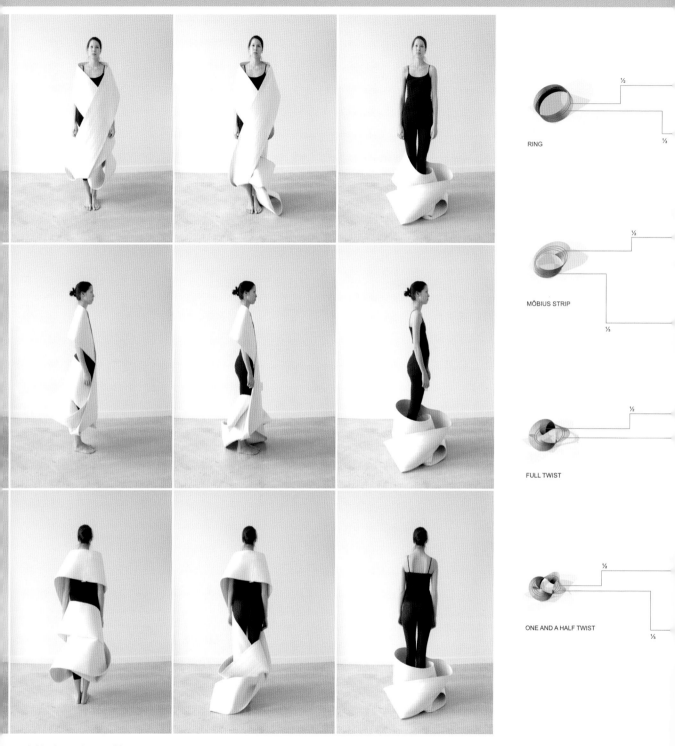

RING

½

⅓

MÖBIUS STRIP

½

⅓

FULL TWIST

½

ONE AND A HALF TWIST

½

⅓

Splitting and unraveling
the MÖBIUS DRESS around
a structuring body
reveals unexpected rela-
tionships between inside
and outside.

This diagram catalogs
a series of loop types
and the relationship of
splitting to knotting,
depending on the origi-
nal topology.

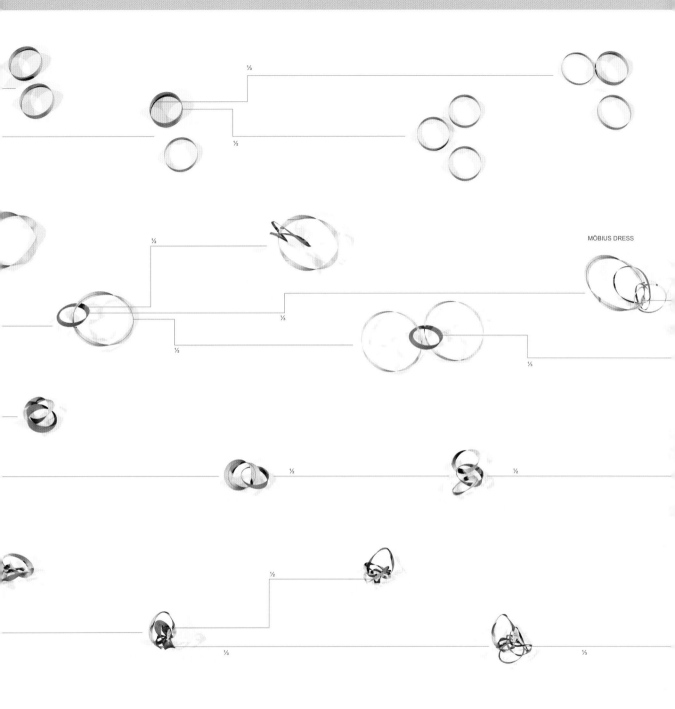

⅓

½

½

⅓

½

MÖBIUS DRESS

⅓

½

½

⅓

½

⅓

The "splitting rule" demonstrates that a strip with an
even number, n, of half twists
creates two loops each with
n half-twists. If n is odd it
creates one loop with 2n + 2
half-twists. Splitting becomes
a generative procedure.

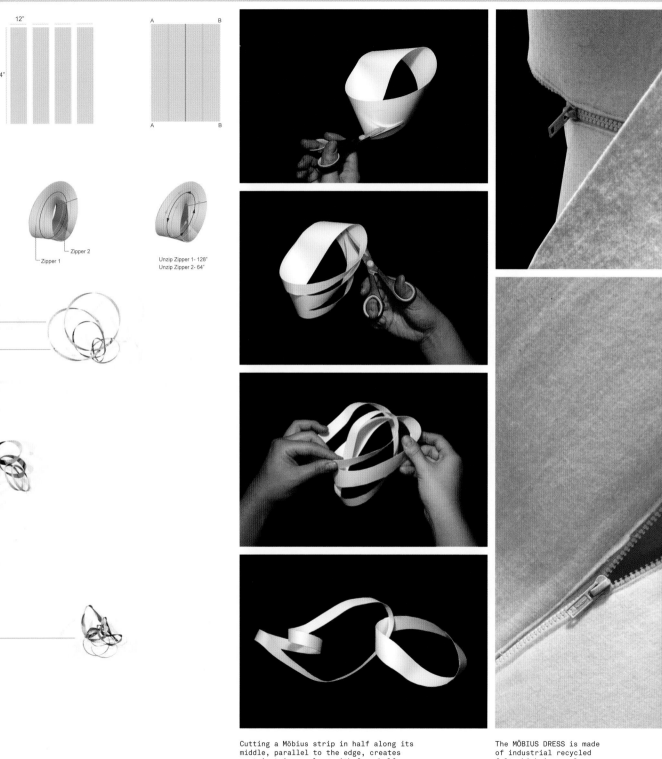

Cutting a Möbius strip in half along its middle, parallel to the edge, creates a strip twice as long with four half twists. Cutting this new loop down the middle creates two strips linked around each other, each with four half twists. Cutting the Möbius strip in thirds creates two linked loops, one with one half twist and one with four half twists.

The MÖBIUS DRESS is made of industrial recycled felt which is seamless and directionless.

12"

64"

A   B

A   B

Zipper 2

Zipper 1

Unzip Zipper 1- 128"
Unzip Zipper 2- 64"

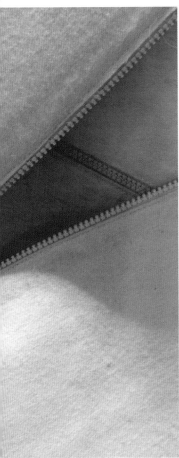

INNER LINER

Between the envelopes of clothing and architecture exist multiple zones of interstitial space. THREE DEGREES OF FELT exploits this physical space between the body and the building to create a nonuniform inner liner to display over four hundred Aztec artifacts. A strategy of creating surplus surface was used to accommodate the large amount of artifacts within the defined perimeter of the rotunda. Undulating in and out of the Guggenheim's structural bay system to increase the linear footage of display, the ribbon wall delaminates to house the various artifacts and structures new spatial relationships between the viewers, artifacts, and existing architecture.

Whereas the Möbius Dress literally unravels around the body, THREE DEGREES OF FELT creates a continuously unfolding micro- and macrospatial sequence along the ramp of the Guggenheim. The project's final form is the result of an elastically responsive logic. The inserted envelope adapts specifically at the scale of the artifact and the overall building structure, pushing and pulling to define a new sequence of spatial experiences.

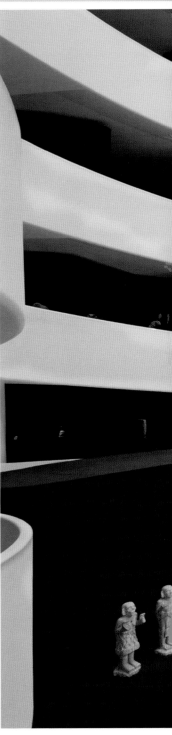

The Aztec Empire exhibition was designed in collaboration with Enrique Norten/TEN Arquitectos (see Project Credits).

The Aztec Empire

The insertion of an interior
liner to accommodate the
majority of Aztec artifacts
temporarily transformed
the visual, acoustical, and
experiential conditions of
the Guggenheim Museum.

This responsive logic begins with an understanding of each object's size, weight, security needs, and ideal relationships to other artifacts and the viewer. Various lenders' loan agreements dictated whether the artifacts were designated for open display, protection behind glass, or containment in environmental vitrines. Exremely heavy artifacts required larger horizontal platforms to spread their load. These "pocket parameters," hardwired into each object, remained constant even as the sequence of objects evolved based on curatorial direction during the planning stages.

Using parametric rules, a series of scripts were applied to produce a reconfigurable geometry for the ribbon wall that incorporated each object's unique constraints. This system yielded the final form of the ribbon wall, which wraps and splits to showcase each object. Absorbing the various visual criteria of display, accommodating the physical load conditions of each artifact, and choreographing a constantly unfolding variable experience, the surplus surface of the ribbon wall is performative.

The inserted wall masks the structural bay system in order to reinforce the experience of the perimeter circulation as gallery. As the bays deepen moving up the ramp of the Guggenheim, the folded ribbon wall transforms to create shallow pockets for the artifacts and larger pockets of space that form semidiscrete gallery spaces within the system of overall folds. On the top ramp level of the rotunda, the liner pulls away from the building structure, bifurcating the circulation space to allow viewers to walk up one side and down the other, resulting in a truly continuous circulation loop. The material choice of half-inch-thick felt for the wall surface further underscores the performative nature of the ribbon wall. By absorbing light and sound, the thick, dark felt of the wall transforms the Guggenheim's white interior into a deep, mute, inverted envelope.

The Aztec Empire exhibition featured over four hundred unique artifacts. In order to accommodate this quantity, the ribbon wall folds in and out of the bays to expand the linear square footage available for display.

Each artifact has a unique
"shelf" that is created by the
gap or pocket of space created
in the delamination of the liner
surface. The various "pockets"
for the artifacts have a smooth
relationship to each other,
allowing the wall to read as a
continuous system.

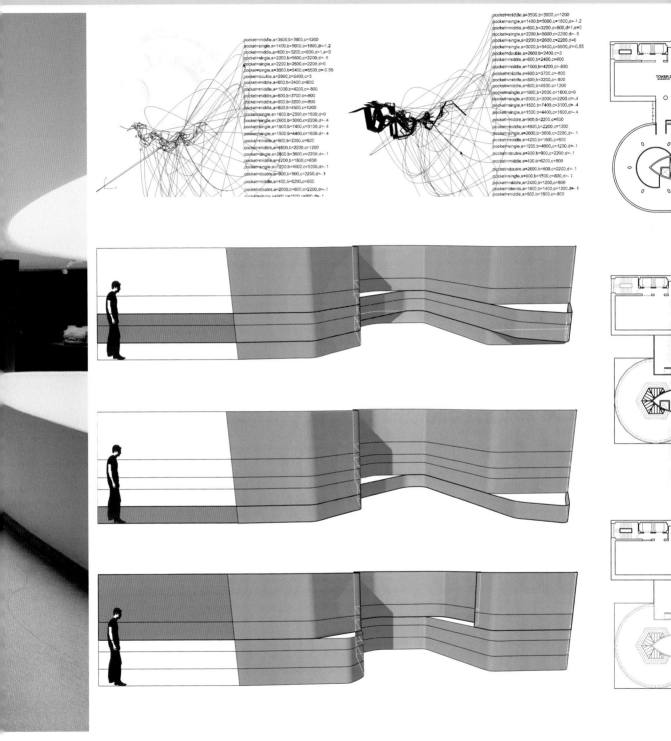

A series of "pocket parameters" were used to generate
the ins, outs, and splits of
the inner envelope. A corresponding series of plug-ins
and scripts link each object
to information on how to
build its specific pocket.

Splits and folds of
the ribbon wall account
for the lines of sight
of the viewer, optimiz-
ing the potential rela-
tionship between object
and subject.

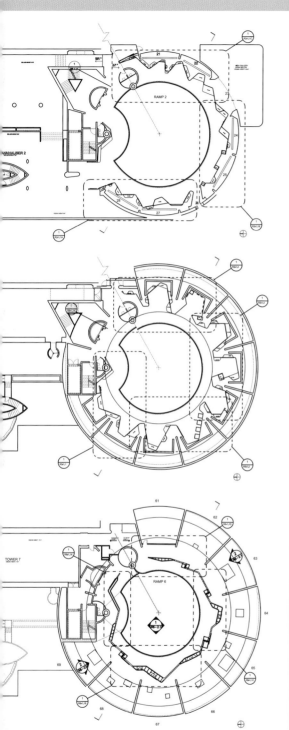

As the bays deepen moving up
the ramp of the Guggenheim, the
ribbon wall transforms from
shallow pockets for objects
to larger alcoves that form
intimate gallery spaces. On the
sixth-floor ramp, the wall moves
toward the center and allows
one to occupy both of its sides.

The ribbon wall transforms
in response to both the
specific artifacts it houses
and the spatial qualities
of each of the six ramps
to create a continuous but
varied experience.

Focusing on the experience
of the perimeter and periphery, as opposed to the
singular center, the surface
creates multiple centers
as one moves through the
rotunda.

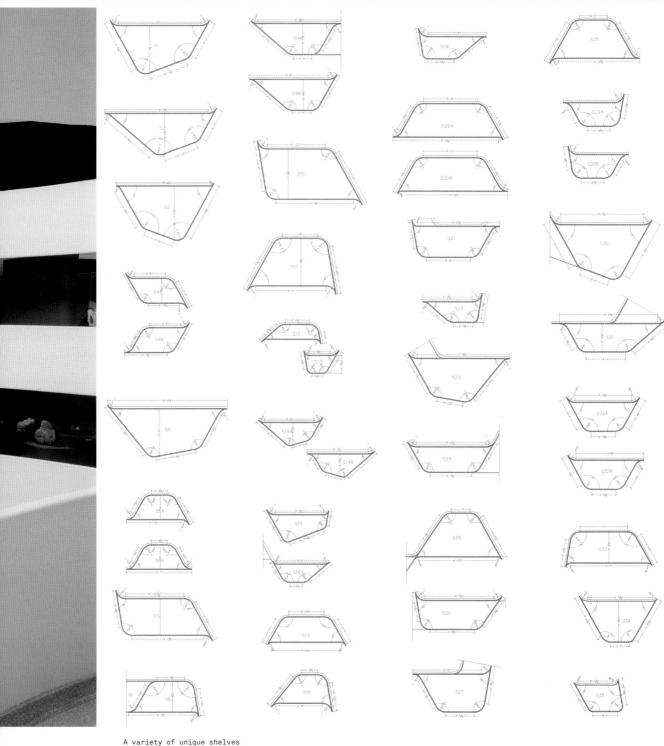

A variety of unique shelves differing in size, shape, and orientation were pre-fabricated. The connecting segments of the ribbon wall were built on-site.

TANGENT SURFACES

The "loose fill" of the PS1 LOOP installation makes a tenuous but tangible connection from skin to skin and surface to surface. At once 100 percent fill and 100 percent void, the continuous and structurally interdependent loops circumscribe cellular volumes, occupying the entire courtyard of the PS1 Contemporary Art Center. By proxy, touching one loop means touching every loop, creating a tangential occupation of one's complete surroundings.

Part landscape and part infrastructure, this pliable latticework acts as an interactive jungle gym, featuring a number of specifically programmed activity clusters including wading pools, waterfalls, bubble jets, and a collective trampoline. Its lower surfaces are sculpted for lounging, while the upper canopy provides shade. Greater porosity facilitates easy passage through the central circulation areas, while greater material density promotes loitering around the periphery.

The geometry of the fill is generated through a three-dimensional Voronoi cell-packing algorithm that, based on principles of proximity, divides a space according to a given set of points. The polypropylene lattice of loops was designed and fabricated using both digital and analog design and modeling techniques. Numerous prototypes were used to test the structural integrity and construction sequence of the interdependent loops and the material properties of polypropylene, including ductility, elasticity, and bending. Utilizing the deflection of the material and the conical section of the biased loops, the installation creates an inhabitable, immersive environment between the scales of furniture and architecture.

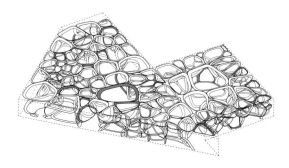

PS1 LOOP creates an immersive condition as a scaffold for activities.

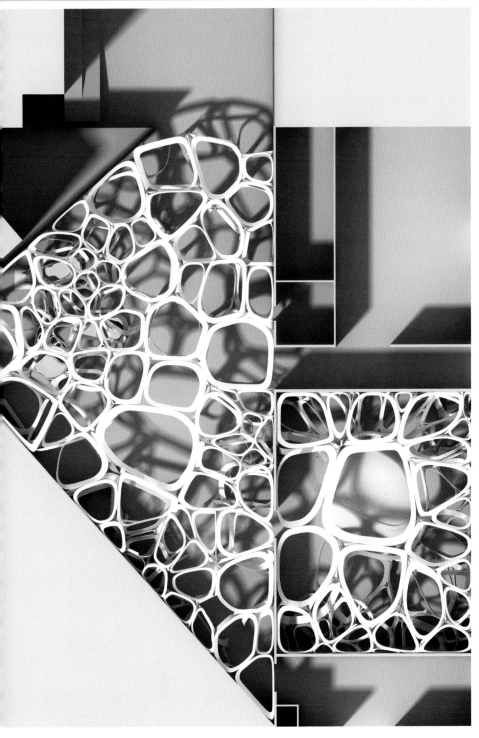

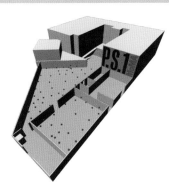

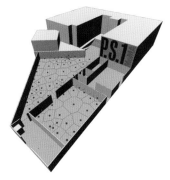

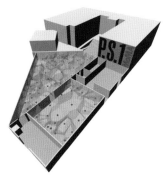

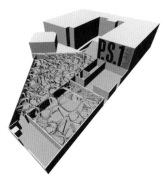

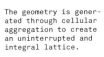

The geometry is gener-
ated through cellular
aggregation to create
an uninterrupted and
integral lattice.

A point cloud based on
program densities was used
to generate the cellular-
packing geometry. A script
modified this geometry into
loops with a conical section
toward the center of each
spherical cell.

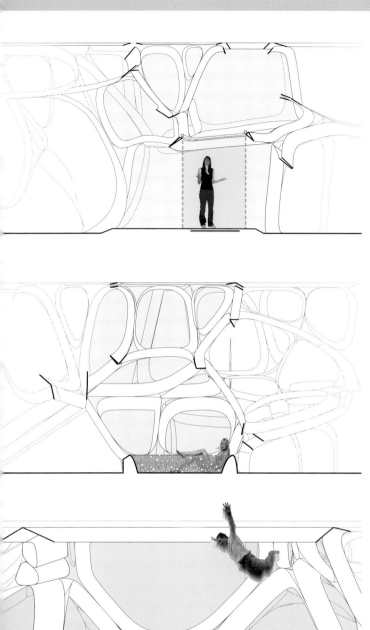

Some of these areas—the waterfalls, foam chamber, and bubble jets—would use motion sensors to automate their activation, allowing PS1 LOOP to respond to its occupants.

PS1 LOOP aspires to be a completely immersive social environment. Through an atmospheric thickening of the ground plane, it provides a dense scaffold for the unpredictable unfolding of social exchange.

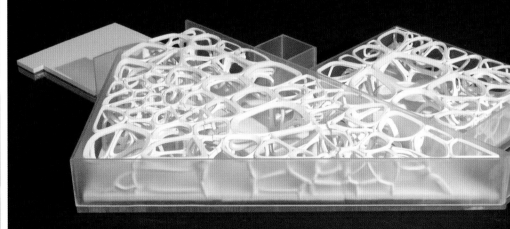

Instead of proposing an architectural installation that would sit within the PS1 courtyard, PS1 LOOP fills the void of the courtyard with an infrastructural landscape.

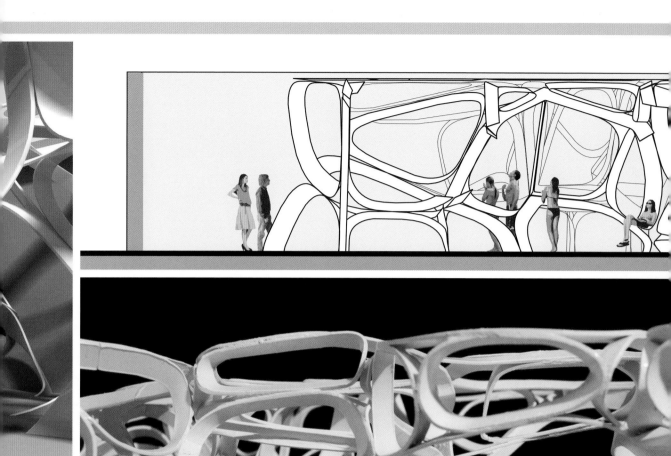

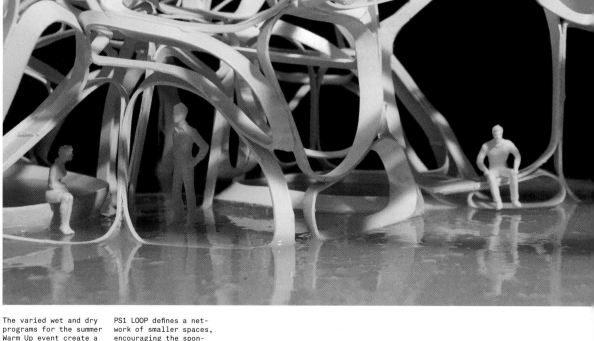

The varied wet and dry programs for the summer Warm Up event create a spectrum of densities within the loose fill.

PS1 LOOP defines a network of smaller spaces, encouraging the spontaneous formation of discrete activity groupings during the Warm Up event.

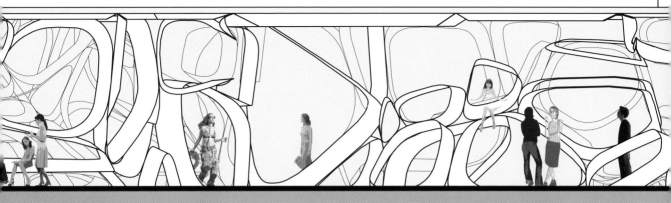

The main components
of PS1 LOOP—the loops
themselves—are designed
and fabricated through
digital processes.

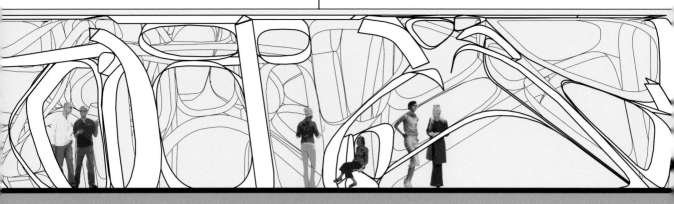

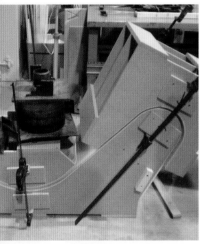

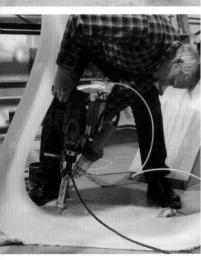

Segments are CNC milled and joined with a plastic welder. Polypropylene is a 100 percent recyclable material that can be welded with polypropylene, as opposed to solvents. The individual loops are mechanically fastened together on-site.

A full-scale prototype was built to test the material and structural properties of the polypropylene loops.

The lower segments are made from a single surface of half-inch-thick polypropylene with one seam. The sheet is heated in an oven and draped around a wooden mold, "clamping" the sheet into its specific form as it cools.

SURFACE INFLECTIONS

The LOOP CHAIRS expand on material investigations initiated by the PS1 LOOP proposal. Scaled down to the order of one body, the material properties, fabrication techniques, and inhabitation of the singular envelope were tested at full scale. Shaped by the body and conceived of as a single closed ribbon, each of the LOOP CHAIRS provides a nested interior and exterior space in which one might sit or recline. Made from polypropylene, each chair is heat-formed over wooden molds and connected with one plastic weld at its seam.

The material properties of the plastic allow for deflection and subtle accommodation of a body's contours and weight. The chair's lightness, thinness, and translucency—along with the gentle deflection of its form when occupied—reinforce an uncanny feeling that one is sitting on air. Creating both an interior and an exterior, LOOP CHAIRS accommodate double occupancy, encouraging two people to share each chair and negotiate its boundary.

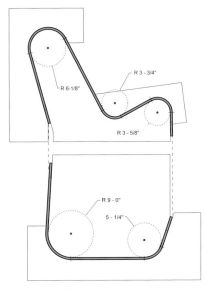

R 3 - 3/4"
R 6-1/8"
R 3 - 5/8"
R 9 - 0"
5 - 1/4"

Several pieces compose each mold. Various radii are calibrated to ensure the material's ability to hold its form.

LOOP CHAIRS consist of a single surface that inscribes interior and exterior modes of inhabitation in various configurations.

Each LOOP CHAIR carries
the load of one body,
deflecting and adjusting
to human weight.

BODY WRAPPERS

Intermediate surfaces negotiate the volume defined between the envelopes of clothing and building. As contemporary practice expands to encompass related disciplines, architectures of the interior create opportunities to explore the relationship between the body and its immediate environment.

TRIO lines the interior envelope of a building while accommodating the body as large-scale furniture, engaging inhabitants through simple bends and folds. TRIO consists of a series of discrete "liner" elements that wrap around the ceiling and wall surfaces of three ground-floor public spaces serving a cluster of condominiums. These "wrapper" elements exist as interstitial membranes, held at a short distance from the building shell. They create thresholds, define zones of activity, and serve as public furniture within the lobby volumes.

Made of COR, an engineered wood material, function of the wrappers is not differentiated through material change, but through form. The wrapping surfaces anticipate and conform to the geometries of the body in a range of positions and activities. Transforming from a bench to a desk to a canopy, the wrapper accomodates various programmatic conditions that interface the body and building.

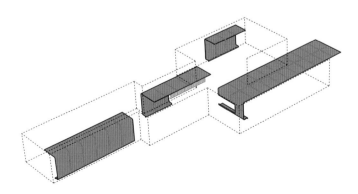

TRIO's surfaces create scenarios for public-space interactions in the three residential lobbies they occupy.

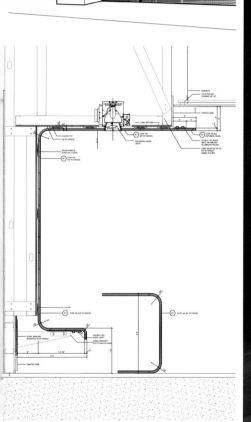

Delineating a continuous surface between the exterior canopy and the lobby's interior, the canopy wrapper creates a smooth transition between outside and inside.

The canopy wrapper bends down to become the front desk, forming the first surface of interface between visitor and concierge.

Creating a continuous bench along the edge of the mailboxes, TRIO encourages social exchange as people linger to get their mail.

The wrapper, hung from the interior wall structure, is detailed to appear as thin as possible while still remaining able to perform its function as an extruded public bench.

THERMAL ENVELOPES

An envelope may act materially, mediating environmental conditions and controlling flow between volumes, as well as formally, responding to and shaping the body's movements and activities. HOTEL ΔT deploys multiple layers of envelope between the body and the environment to establish varying conditioned zones between wet and dry programs. Consequently, the project forms a series of thermal and spatial envelopes that create microconditions for the body.

Beginning with a careful understanding of the body and its needs with respect to the mixed typology of a hotel/spa, the project expands to include the formal, spatial, and atmospheric characteristics of each program. Accommodating its multiple offerings, HOTEL ΔT houses several varying thermal environments and conditional gradients (wet to dry, hot to cold, public to private) by wrapping envelopes within envelopes. Interior layers accommodate an array of ergonomic functions: fully reclined, partially reclined, upright, or standing.

The outermost envelope, a double-skin cavity facade, modulates temperature across the south face while providing clear views out to the water. Within the cavity, the heated air is vented out and recuperated, while operable sun shading is adjusted to screen out light or bounce light in. This facade system allows the building to perform more efficiently and sets up a strategic series of layers from the guest room to the spa. These envelopes enable multiple interior microclimates, transforming the perceptual and sensorial experience of the architectural environment. HOTEL ΔT explores performative potentials of surface logics by manipulating surfaces in the service of bodily comfort and atmospheric modulation.

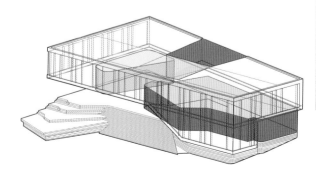

COR, an engineered wood product, is used to create the wrappers. Working with the manufacturer of the material, TRIO tests the limits of radii and load.

The occupiable ground-floor level is set fifteen feet above the mean high-water line by regulation. The spa programs occupy this first floor, with the hotel rooms above and the public deck within the floodplain zone.

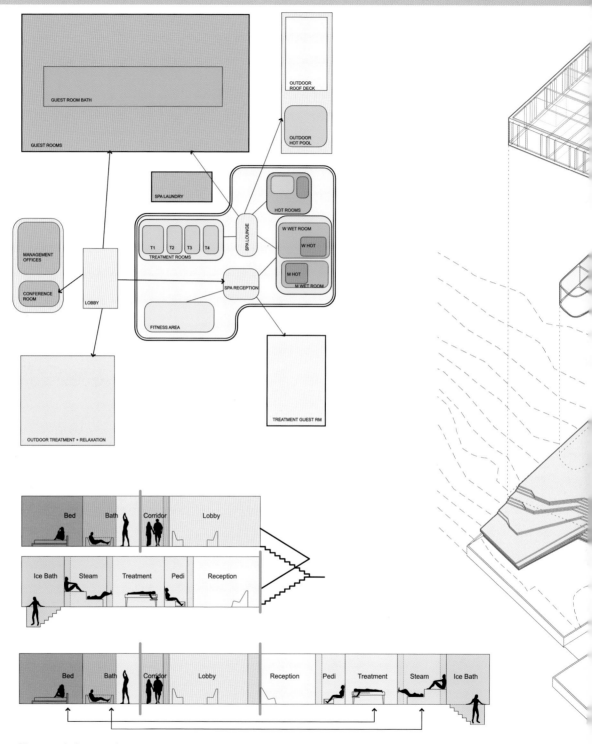

Diagrams of the wet and
dry program relation-
ships in the hotel and
spa study the thermal
conditions of each pro-
gram element, desired
adjacencies, and thermal
requirements.

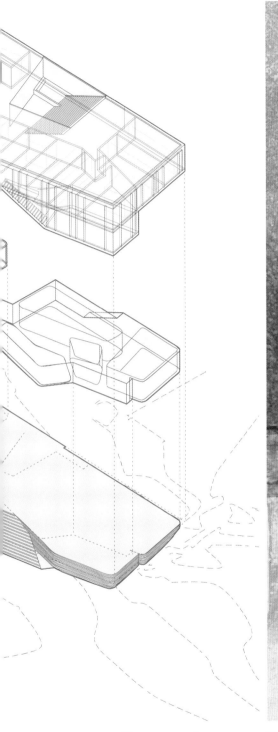

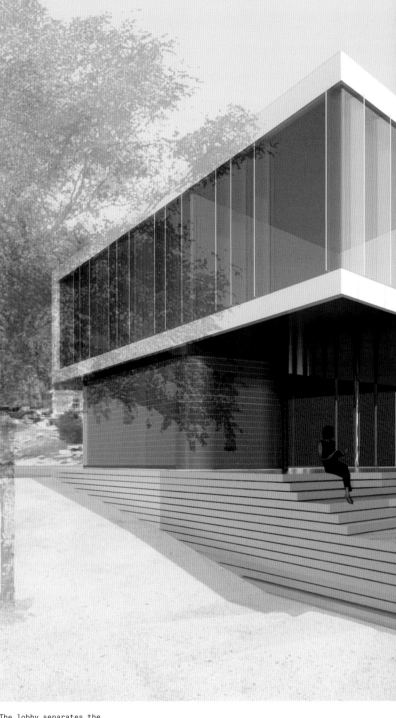

The spa program is organized as a series of envelopes within envelopes that regulate microenvironments within the building.

The lobby separates the discreet hotel programs from the spa program on the ground floor. The nested envelopes differentiate various internal spa program areas.

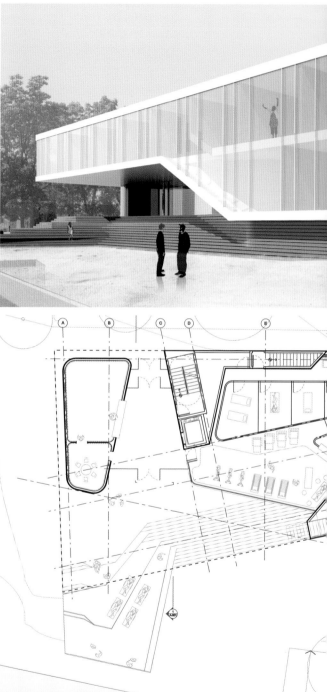

The hotel volume above shades the public deck, where various activities related to the public/private hotel lobby and the spa occur.

The "back" facade is also the "front," facing the water. The terraced decking and hotel volume sandwich the spa program between two articulated volumes.

The building massing is negotiated between the "grandfathered" footprint of the existing building and the fifty-foot Coastal Resource Management setback line from the water's edge.

CRMC
SET BACK LINE

Interior and exterior envelopes define programmatic zones based on functional, experiential, and atmospheric affinities.

The second-floor plan accommodates thirteen private rooms that vary in terms of wet and dry program ratios. A sauna on the second floor ties into the spa program on the first floor.

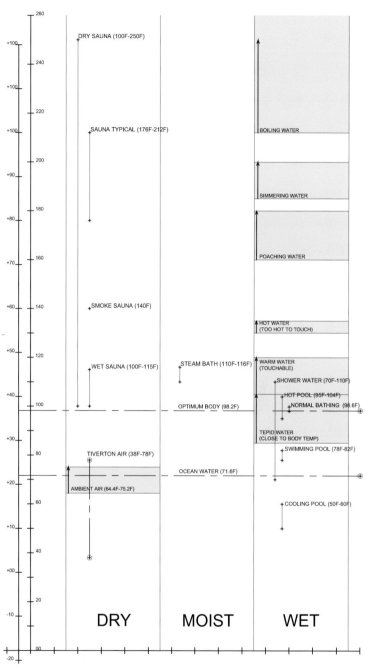

DRY MOIST WET

260
+100 240
+100 220
+100 200
+90 180
+80 160
+70 140
+60 120
+50 100
+40 80
+30 60
+20 40
+10 20
+00 00
-10
-20

DRY SAUNA (100F-250F)
SAUNA TYPICAL (176F-212F)
SMOKE SAUNA (140F)
WET SAUNA (100F-115F)
TIVERTON AIR (38F-78F)
AMBIENT AIR (64.4F-75.2F)

STEAM BATH (110F-116F)
OPTIMUM BODY (98.2F)
OCEAN WATER (71.6F)

BOILING WATER
SIMMERING WATER
POACHING WATER
HOT WATER (TOO HOT TO TOUCH)
WARM WATER (TOUCHABLE)
SHOWER WATER (70F-110F)
HOT POOL (95F-104F)
NORMAL BATHING (98.6F)
TEPID WATER (CLOSE TO BODY TEMP)
SWIMMING POOL (78F-82F)
COOLING POOL (50F-60F)

A graph organizes the thermal range of various program elements into dry, moist, and wet conditions.

25% WET 75% DRY

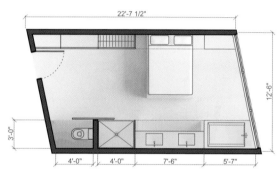

22'-7 1/2"
12'-6"
3'-0"
4'-0" 4'-0" 7'-6" 5'-7"

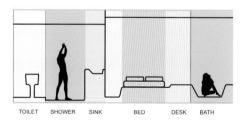

TOILET SHOWER SINK BED DESK BATH

Three types of guest rooms are available. Differentiated by ratios of wet to dry, the room options organize the programs into parallel bands.

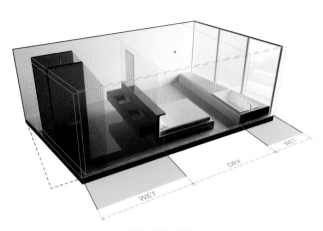

50% WET 50% DRY

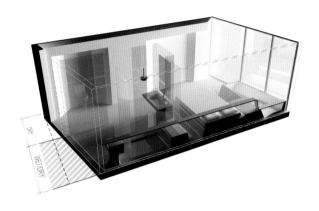

70% WET 30% DRY

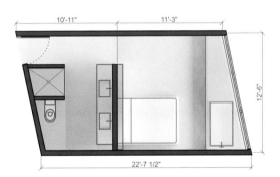

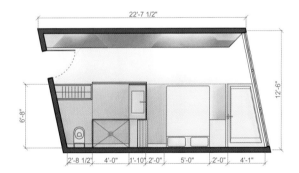

SHOWER   SINK   BED   BATH

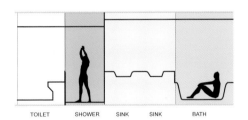

TOILET   SHOWER   SINK   SINK   BATH

Negotiating the con-
ceptual space between
furniture and archi-
tecture, continu-
ous surfaces conform
to an array of body
positions.

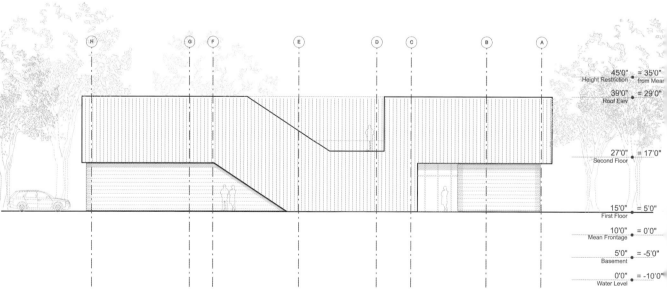

H	G	F	E	D	C	B	A

45'0" = 35'0"
Height Restriction from Mean

39'0" = 29'0"
Roof Elev

27'0" = 17'0"
Second Floor

15'0" = 5'0"
First Floor

10'0" = 0'0"
Mean Frontage

5'0" = -5'0"
Basement

0'0" = -10'0"
Water Level

Surface articulation
differentiates the exte-
rior envelopes of the
building. The street
facade is more opaque
than the waterfront
facade.

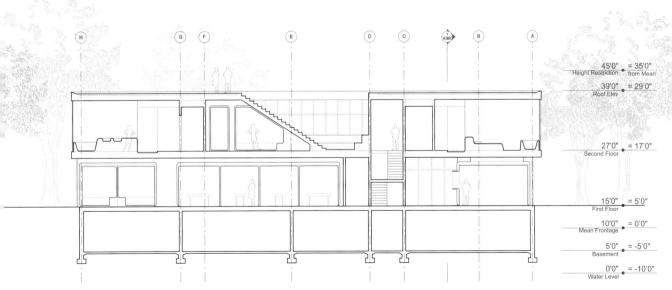

A public roof terrace on
the second floor accom-
modates exterior shared
spa and hotel programs.

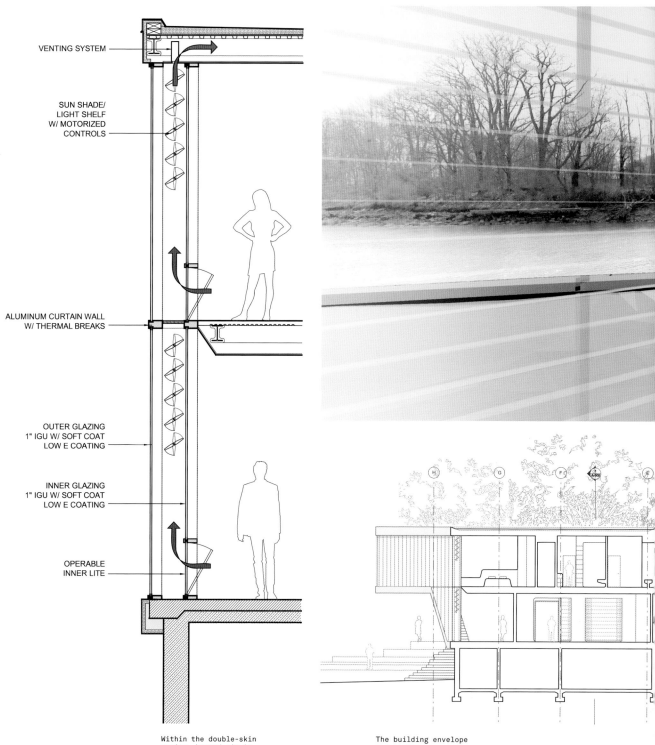

VENTING SYSTEM

SUN SHADE/
LIGHT SHELF
W/ MOTORIZED
CONTROLS

ALUMINUM CURTAIN WALL
W/ THERMAL BREAKS

OUTER GLAZING
1" IGU W/ SOFT COAT
LOW E COATING

INNER GLAZING
1" IGU W/ SOFT COAT
LOW E COATING

OPERABLE
INNER LITE

Within the double-skin
cavity, heated air is
vented out and recuper-
ated. Operable sun shading
louvers adjust to screen
out light or bounce light
into the space.

The building envelope
negotiates the condi-
tions between inside and
outside. Single surface
elements within the guest
rooms and spa mediate wet
and dry differences while
providing continuity
among them.

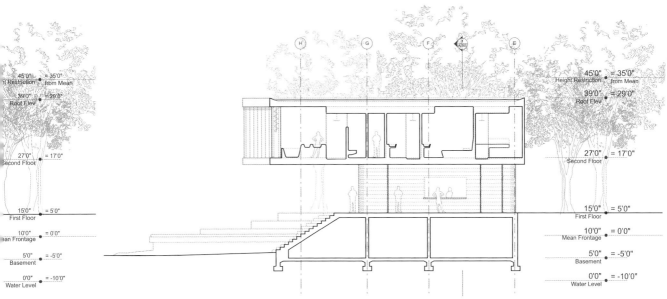

A double-skin cavity facade modulates temperature across the south face while providing clear views out to the water.

The hotel program is articulated as a contained volume that sits on the spa elements. The building negotiates the section, allowing public access to the waterfront through or alongside the building.

The ground floor permits
access from the street
level to the waterfront
deck, allowing the land-
scape to slip through.

NATURES

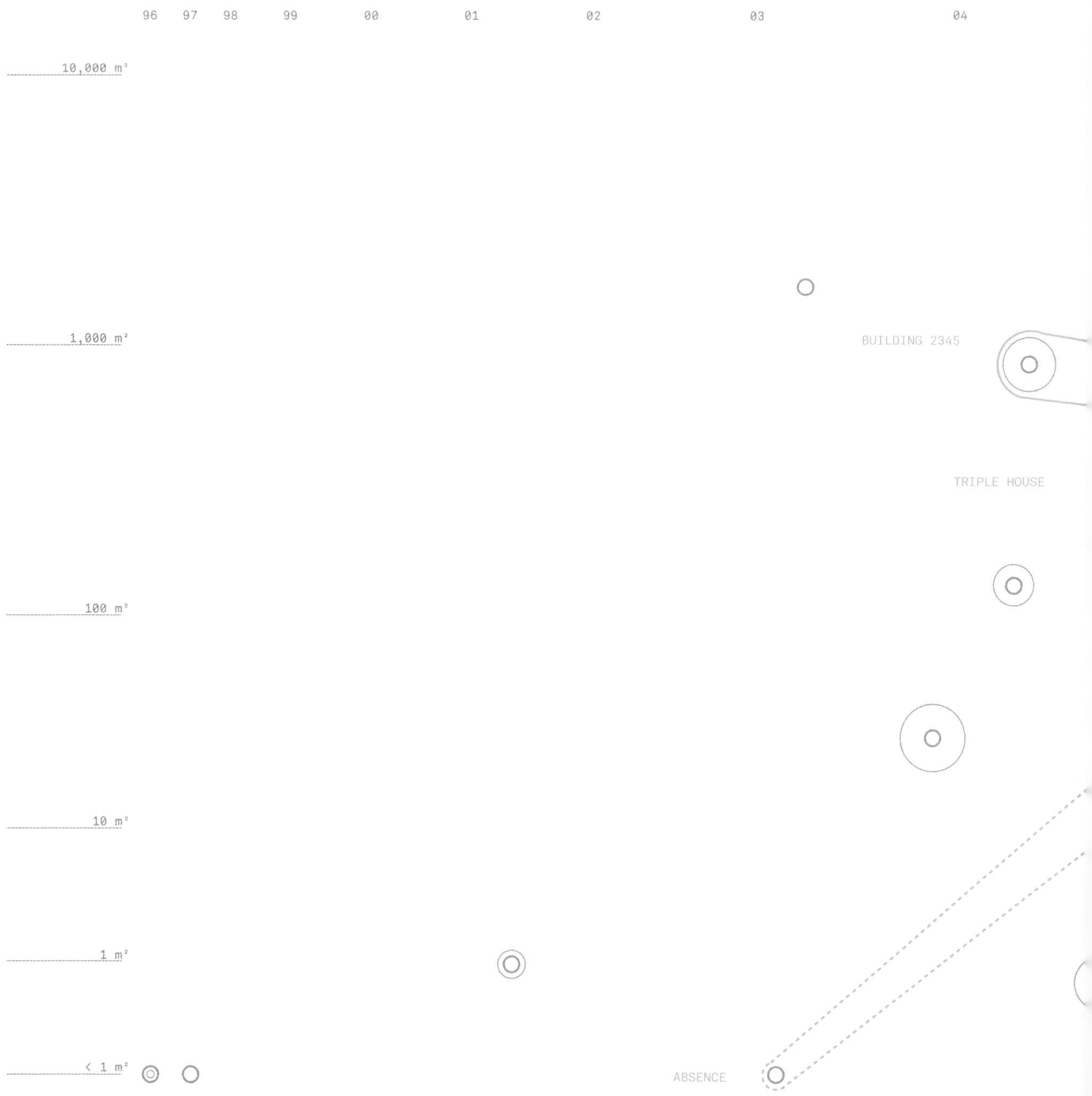

96
97
98
99
00
01
02
03
04
10,000 m²
1,000 m²
BUILDING 2345
TRIPLE HOUSE
100 m²
10 m²
1 m²
< 1 m²
ABSENCE

05   06   07   08

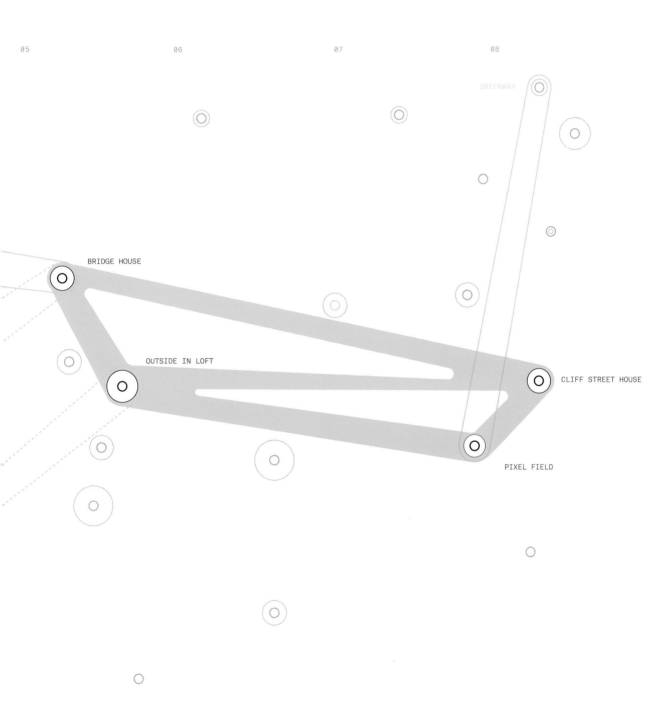

GREENWAY

BRIDGE HOUSE

OUTSIDE IN LOFT

CLIFF STREET HOUSE

PIXEL FIELD

From the microscopic scale of nanomaterials to the global scale of climate change, the definitions of and relationships between the "artificial" and the "natural" are continuously being recalibrated. We understand our environment as being always already marked by human presence, where the natural is contingent on its relationship to the artificial. At the architectural scale, relationships between the artificial and the natural are equally complex and multivalent. Architecture by definition intervenes in the world, reconfiguring the status of the natural. Architecture alters "natural" conditions, contours, and ecosystems, domesticating its contexts and transforming the open and "wild" into controlled and conditioned space.

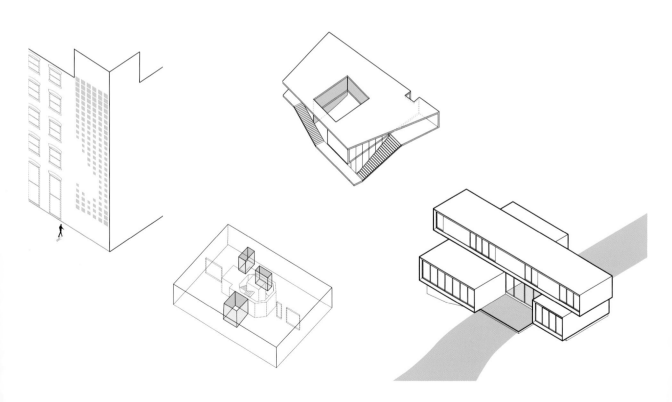

Our contemporary cultural context forces us to revise our definition of nature as something that is relative and contingent as opposed to absolute. We must also recognize that nature, or the natural, is actively produced—naturalized. Architecture can act as a domesticating device, as a normalizing or naturalizing agent. Through comparative and active engagement with the domestic's other, the uncanny, our research takes on a syntactic rather than semantic character. We define concepts by their inverse—understanding nature and architecture, the domestic and the uncanny, as partners in the construction of our environment.[1]

In the context of domesticity, sites of "nature" are often associated with an idealized pastoral precondition to the quintessential architectural artifact: the suburban home. The "natural site" becomes the foreground to and the backdrop of the house. It is both the necessary context for the house and also its antithesis; the yard is an idealized and domesticated landscape, while a panoramic view of the landscape is the prized object of architecture's contemplative gaze. In her essay "Unbreathed Air 1956," historian Beatriz Colomina ultimately identifies Alison and Peter Smithson's House of the Future—including its central garden—as a hole. Rather than boring a courtyard into the center of a home, the House of the Future wraps itself around a void, guarding the pristine air it offers its inhabitants.[2] For the Smithsons and for Colomina, "nature" precedes the House of the Future.

The OUTSIDE IN LOFT is similar to the Smithson house in that it invites three volumes of the outside into the interior domestic space. The courtyard literally brings the exterior in, inviting natural phenomena into an urban apartment. While the architecture does not control the rain, snow, or sleet, it wraps around the weather to frame it in a cubic volume, naturalizing it within a domestic interior landscape.

CLIFF STREET HOUSE also engages in the active construction of relationships with its "natural" context. Sited in an extreme, sloping landscape, the project creates a courtyard within the house as a level zone within the dramatic topography, giving the site a momentary yard. Further complicating the interplay between landscape and architecture, this single-family dwelling accommodates a preexisting public path into the private home. Connecting a road at the top of the hill to a state park at the bottom of the slope, the project reads as both introverted and extroverted, folding back on itself as public circulation wraps around it. By incorporating the courtyard and the path into the home, the project addresses the possible conflations between architecture, infrastructure, and landscape at a domestic scale.

BRIDGE HOUSE examines architecture as a framing device for landscape. The structure spans a zone of suburban landscape that slips from the front yard to the back yard, passing through the domestic scene. A gradient of hard and soft surfaces form a material index of the site. This designated core sample of "nature," around which the house is structured, expands the occupant's gaze from outside to inside to outside again.

The framing or reframing of landscape in relation to architecture is further studied through PIXEL FIELD. The notion of the uncanny is evoked in this reoriented landscape. Rendered explicitly artificial, this project prompts the viewer to question the usual associations of natural and artificial, green and urban. PIXEL FIELD's vertical orientation and its pixelated pattern each demonstrate the simultaneous but polar drives of wildness and domestication. Rotating the assumed orientation of a landscape by 90 degrees, the plant matter is grown vertically, using a lightweight engineered-soil medium. This artificial landscape contains "nature" in a format usually reserved for digital media—the pixelated gradient.

The projects included in this chapter engage basic organizing principles of the contemporary landscape, problematizing assumptions regarding the relationship between nature and architecture. They illustrate an approach closely attuned to the syntax of these themes and their relationships to each other, as opposed to a singular attitude toward nature and the environment. These strategies seek to reconfigure the normative relationships between figure and ground, inside and outside, vertical and horizontal, in order to challenge our preconceptions of architecture's role in the production of the "natural."

1. See Anthony Vidler, The Architectural Uncanny: Essays in the Modern Unhomely (Cambridge, MA: MIT Press, 1992).
2. Beatriz Colomina, Domesticity at War (Cambridge, MA: MIT Press, 2007), 230.

LIVE MEDIA

The impact of human action on the environment has ensured that all sites are in some way marked by our presence. Given this post-pastoral context, the natural is contingent on its relationship to the artificial and the status of "wilderness" is recalibrated by the "urban." Whereas wilderness suggests a precondition of the urban, contemporary suburban expansion and the permeation of the man-made into all territories forces us to rethink the status of the "wild" in relation to the domesticating force of human activity. The simultaneity of wildness and domestication—typically assumed to be in opposition—is expressed in the dual nature of PIXEL FIELD.

By transforming the orientation and the pattern of a Sedum surface, PIXEL FIELD demonstrates the redeployment of the "wild" in a highly "domesticated" configuration. The rotation of the field from horizontal to vertical questions basic assumptions about the groundedness of plant material. The plant matter grows through a lightweight engineered-soil medium of half-inch-thick felt substrate, which is cut into panels—or pixels—and suspended in front of the building facade. The transformation of the field into a pixel pattern—a format usually reserved for digital media—underscores the artifice of the "new natural."

The PIXEL FIELD's ability to flourish despite its unnatural configuration demonstrates the resilience of the organic matter. The reconfigured field as pattern suggests broader and distributed applications, where the vertical landscape could occupy multiple sites throughout the city.

The project recasts urban architectural interventions as the production of environments that deploy a full range of mineral and vegetal materials to engage with the public through physical encounters with new landscapes, in a larger debate about architecture and the environment. The prototype illustrates how blank urban surfaces can become opportunities for zero footprint public art that improves the city, visually and performatively.

"Parti Wall, Hanging Green" was a collaborative project with Ground, Merge Architects, MOS, over,under, SsD, Studio Luz, UNI, LinOldham Office, and Utile.

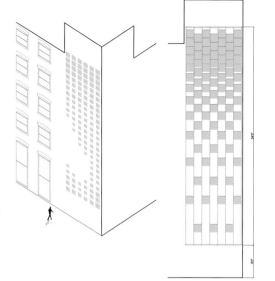

24" Horizontal
Vertical Varies
8 Cables
84 Panels

24" Horizontal
36" Vertical (Running)
8 Cables
115 Panels

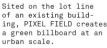

Sited on the lot line of an existing building, PIXEL FIELD creates a green billboard at an urban scale.

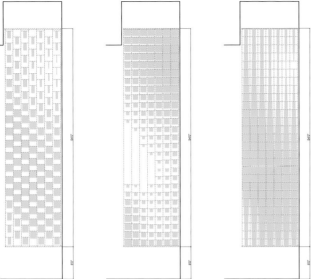

24" Horizontal
36" Vertical (Running)
8 Cables
123 Panels

24" Horizontal
24" Vertical
8 Cables
168 Panels

24" Horizontal
24" Vertical
8 Cables
189 Panels

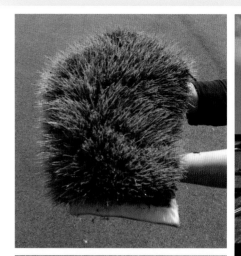

The live media is adapted from a green roof system. The growth medium is rooted in a substrate of plastic woven netting and felt. Individual green pixels are organized by size in the parking lot during installation.

PIXEL FIELD's graphic pattern creates a green gradient along the brick face of its host building. Pattern studies test different gradients.

While Sedum was used in the final installation, earlier studies tested Annual Rye and Chia growth on felt substrates.

Individual panels
hang from stainless
steel cables held in
tension at top
and bottom.

CUBIC YARDS

A desire to bring the natural world, or elements of it, into a domestic space finds precedents across history and geography. Basic questions of method and motive arise: how and why would one invite entropy into the home? How do nature and domesticity cohabitate in an urban setting? In the top floor of an urban building, "nature" finds its point of entry through the renovation of two conjoined apartments. OUTSIDE IN LOFT pulls the exterior in, encapsulating it in three distinct voids excavated from the interior domestic space. Air, precipitation, and light enter the interior of the apartments, providing access to the exterior around the central core of the two units and joining them into one.

Giving over a piece of the domestic interior to the exterior invites the outside in, resulting in predictable advantages as its services enhance the domestic environment: fresh air enters the space not only through its outermost skin but intravenously. A family member can step outside without having to walk down six flights of stairs to the ground floor. Natural light, rain, snow, and fog enter the space, indexing time of day and atmospheric conditions within the landlocked programs of the core. Illuminated by daylight, these three volumes serve adjacent spaces, minimizing the need for electrical lighting during the day.

Measures taken to control and modulate nature's arrival have less predictable advantages. The "wet" spaces of the apartment gravitate inwards toward the service core. Their reconfigured pipes and conduits burrow beneath the floorboards, creating a new interior topography. Interfaces between interior and exterior spaces provide opportunities for material articulation. Mahogany boards slip from inside to outside, lining the kitchen, courtyard, and roof deck above. The internalized exterior volumes create an urban domestic landscape alternative to the front, side, and back yards.

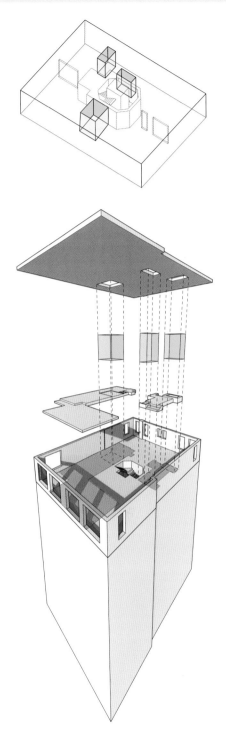

Three aperatures
to the sky and three
incisions into a struc-
tural wall unify the
two apartments into one.

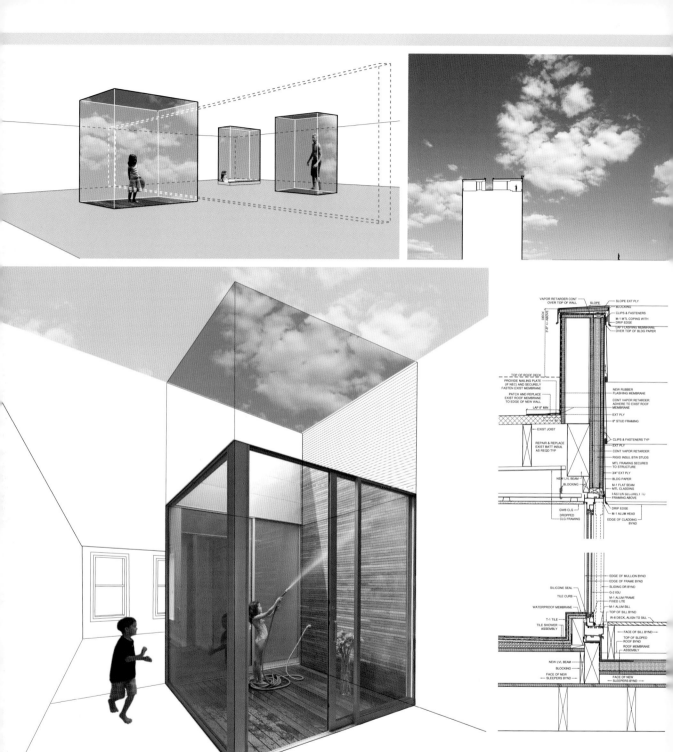

The following labels appear in the construction detail drawings (top detail):

VAPOR RETARDER CONT
OVER TOP OF WALL
SLOPE EXT PLY
SLOPE
BLOCKING
CLIPS & FASTENERS
M-1 MTL COPING WITH
DRIP EDGE
LAP FLASHING MEMBRANE
OVER TOP OF BLDG PAPER

DECK
2'-0" +/- ABOVE

TOP OF ROOF DECK
PROVIDE NAILING PLATE
(IF NEC) AND SECURELY
FASTEN EXIST MEMBRANE
PATCH AND REPLACE
EXIST ROOF MEMBRANE
TO EDGE OF NEW WALL
LAP 8" MIN
EXIST JOIST
REPAIR & REPLACE
EXIST BATT INSUL
AS REQD TYP
NEW LVL BEAM
BLOCKING
GWB CLG
DROPPED
CLG FRAMING

NEW RUBBER
FLASHING MEMBRANE
CONT VAPOR RETARDER:
ADHERE TO EXIST ROOF
MEMBRANE
EXT PLY
6" STUD FRAMING
CLIPS & FASTENERS TYP
EXT PLY
CONT VAPOR RETARDER
RIGID INSUL BTW STUDS
MTL FRAMING SECURED
TO STRUCTURE
3/4" EXT PLY
BLDG PAPER
M-1 FLAT SEAM
MTL CLADDING
FASTEN SECURELY TO
FRAMING ABOVE
DRIP EDGE
M-1 ALUM HEAD
EDGE OF CLADDING
BYND

Lower detail labels:

EDGE OF MULLION BYND
EDGE OF FRAME BYND
G-2 IGU
SLIDING DR BYND
M-1 ALUM FRAME
FIXED LITE
M-1 ALUM SILL
TOP OF SILL BYND
W-6 DECK, ALIGN TO SILL
FACE OF SILL BYND
TOP OF SLOPED
ROOF BYND
ROOF MEMBRANE
ASSEMBLY
FACE OF NEW
SLEEPERS BYND

SILICONE SEAL
TILE CURB
WATERPROOF MEMBRANE
T-1 TILE
TILE SHOWER
ASSEMBLY
NEW LVL BEAM
BLOCKING
FACE OF NEW
SLEEPERS BYND

The courtyard creates an unexpected and unfamiliar outdoor space within the urban apartment's interior. New sets of relationships between inside and outside emerge.

A section, at top, reveals that the sky is brought down into the interior of the loft.

The requirements for the courtyard drainage set the levels for the interior floor and decking. The courtyard drainage connects to the building's existing roof drain.

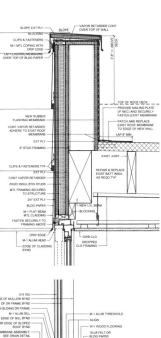

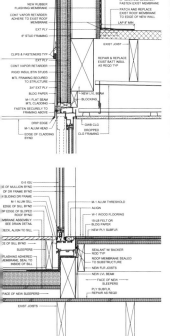

The open-air courtyard connects the loft's interior to its surrounding urban skyline. Cross ventilation and stack effects maximize natural ventilation.

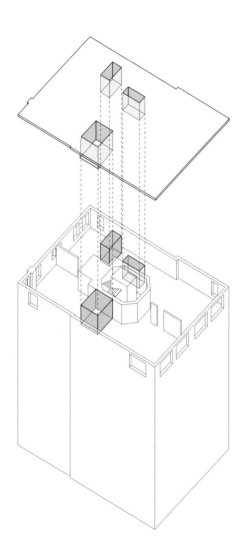

The three cubes of nature
are organized around
the central core of the
building, bringing day-
light into a previously
dark area.

Acid-etched glass sur-
faces provide privacy
to the bath and shower
volumes while allowing
daylight to reach adja-
cent rooms.

Sliding doors on both
sides of the courtyard
link the space to circulation routes, allowing one
to move from inside to
outside to inside again.

The mahogany wood used in
the kitchen and the courtyard will weather to a
natural silver grey on the
exterior while remaining
closer to its original hue
on the interior.

The plan is organized to
create redundant parallel
paths within the apartment.
Circulation moves through the
master bathroom from the front
study to the back bedroom
hallway, treating the bathroom
as an open public thruway in
the apartment.

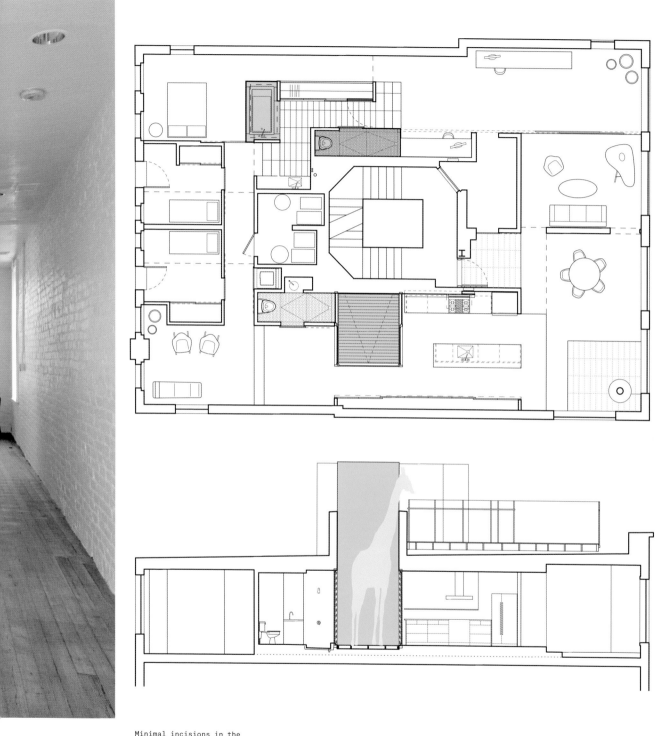

Minimal incisions in the
structural partition
wall join two units into
one. Concentric circula-
tion loops connect the
separate program spaces
of the apartment.

Daylight from the bathtub volume is shared with the hallway and bathroom.

The shower borrows natural light from the courtyard, while the courtyard provides natural ventilation through the apartment.

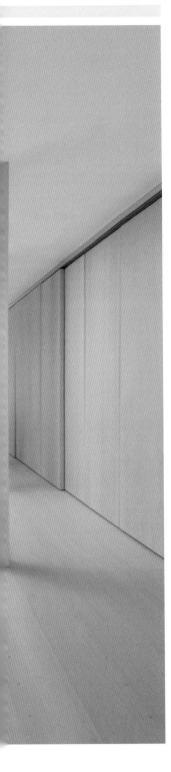

INFLECTED EASEMENT

Land, among the most stable and enduring of resources, often provokes debates over ownership, access, and tenure. A landscape that appears benign, neutral, and undivided may in fact be marked by multiple zones of domain, crossed by rights of way, and intended for a variety of uses. CLIFF STREET HOUSE—which weaves a public path down to a state park through private property—offers a solution to the negotiation of multiple programmatic needs within one parcel of land.

The challenging nature of the site—a steep hill overlooking a gorge—invites further ingenuity. The residence nestles into the hillside as it wraps the path cutting through its site. The resulting form appears both introverted and extroverted, folding back on itself as public circulation moves alongside it. The house surrounds a volume of open landscape that provides a private exterior to the residents. Horizontal wooden panels emphasize the continuously folding form, transitioning from interior to exterior and back again.

Incorporating the path into the home as opposed to relegating it to the site's periphery addresses the infrastructural potential of landscape. Further, it postulates that an infrastructural function need not preclude private use, even within the same site. This modestly scaled proposal indicates the design potentials for negotiating a public easement through a private residence.

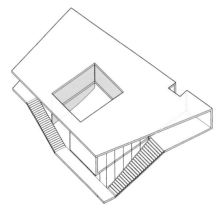

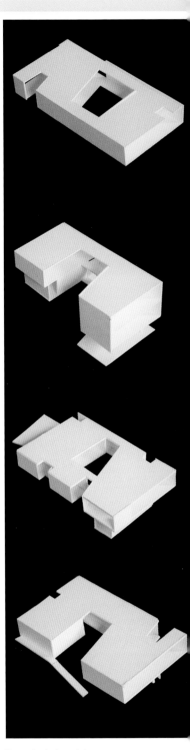

Several study models examine the public path and its relationiship to a more private internal courtyard in the house.

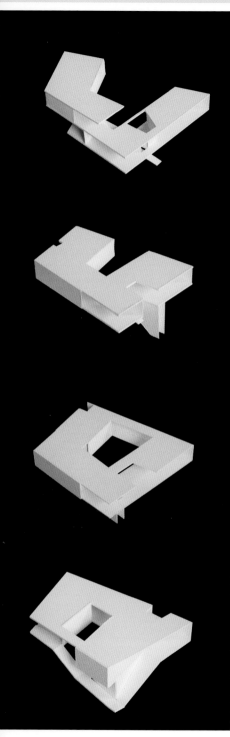

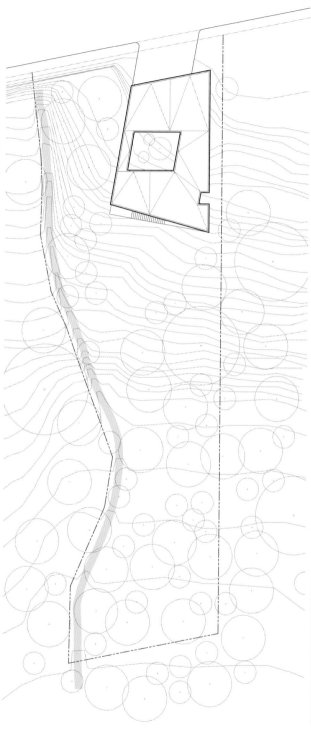

The house frames and contains a volume of nature within its form. A courtyard creates a usable internal yard despite the dramatic slope of the site.

Located on the edge of a gorge, a path along the site is used by residents and visitors to access the state park below.

Perched at the top of
the gorge, the house's
inflected geometry nego-
tiates the dramatic
sectional drop in the
topography.

The surface of the first
floor inflects to create
a public access stair
that follows the section
of the site and wraps
back up to the first-floor
volume of the house.

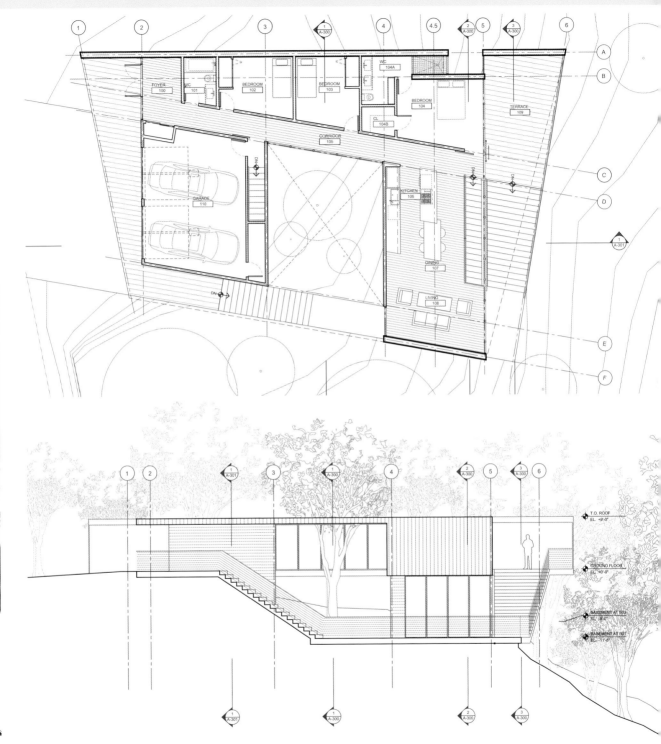

The house creates two circulation bands parallel in plan that split in section. One moves down the hill; the other moves alongside the bedrooms toward the public programs of the house.

Framed by nature, the kitchen and family room volume overlooks the expansive site as well as the internal wrapped courtyard.

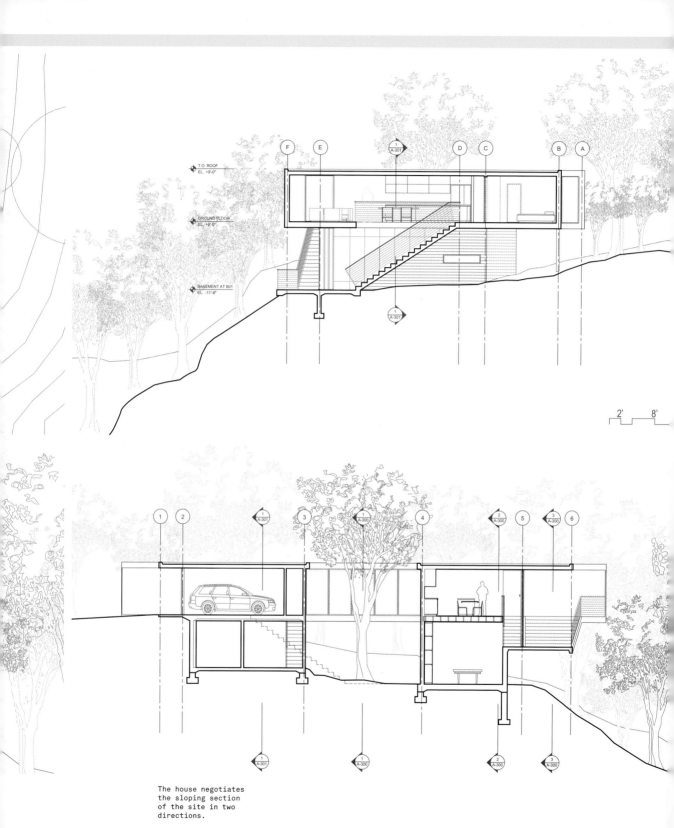

The house negotiates
the sloping section
of the site in two
directions.

The house perches on
the vertical landscape
overlooking Cass Park
and Cayuga Lake.

As pedestrians move along the publicly accessible path to the park, they see the landscape beyond framed through the domestic interior.

ALLÉE

The etymological roots of "landscape" lie in the Dutch tradition of image-making and framing in landscape painting. In contexts of suburbia, landscape is often used as a blanket term referring to the standard lawn and hedges into which homes are indiscriminately tucked. BRIDGE HOUSE focuses on the critical as well as colloquial meanings of landscape as related to its suburban site and domestic program.

Natural elements surrounding a home are as often framers of views as they are framed by views. A front lawn, for example, choreographs views of the house from the street and vice versa, acting as a two-way framing device. This pattern is symmetrically repeated behind the house with the backyard, the house itself drawing a clear barrier through the suburban landscape, dividing a site's front and back.

BRIDGE HOUSE spans the literal divide between its front and back yards as well as the historical and conceptual gap between the tradition of framing in landscape painting and the colloquial understanding of landscape as nature. Three extruded forms compose BRIDGE HOUSE. Two lower parallel volumes define a central view through the house while supporting a perpendicular bridging upper volume. Collectively, these three volumes frame a central landscape zone whose continuity is underscored by its ground-plane materiality— grass gives way to Grasscrete, then concrete, then turns to grass again. Each volume frames its own view, which is emphasized by a smooth, telescopic exterior surface of zinc metal panels, whose beveled profiles situate the suburban landscape within a new frame.

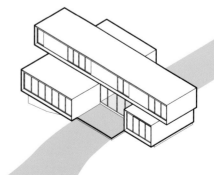

The house is seen as a framing device. The four rooms in the upper volume enjoy unobstructed views while the neighbors gaze through the house to the landscape beyond.

BRIDGE HOUSE creates a see-through condition from the front yard to the back yard by elevating the second floor above the separated ground-floor programs.

The site plan shows the
required setback and
the location of BRIDGE
HOUSE relative to the
Resource Protection
Area of the lot.

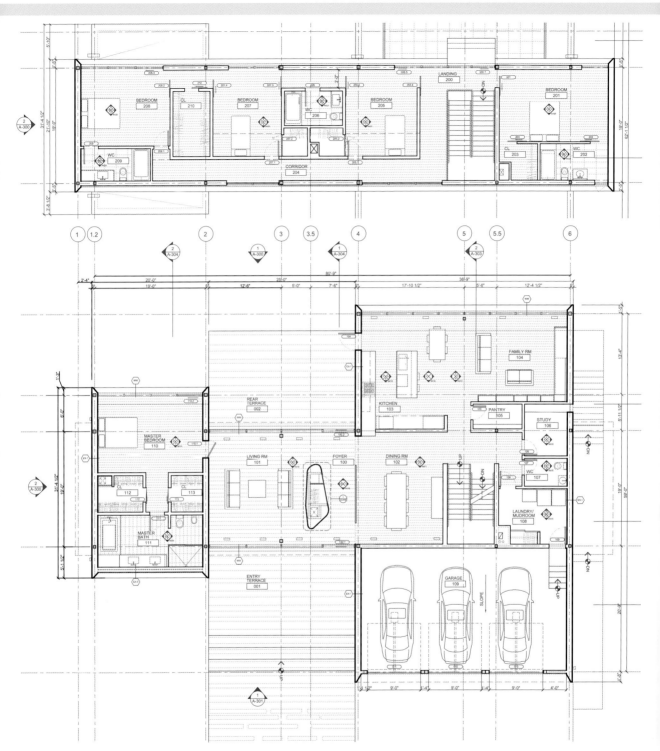

The upper volume's
four bedrooms are
organized as an enfi-
lade along the glazed
facade and are con-
nected by a hallway
on the other side.

The ground floor is divided
into two volumes that support the bridging volume
above. The intermediate
living room pulls the lawn
through the interior of
the house.

The front lawn slips
through the house, cre-
ating continuity from
outside to inside back
to outside.

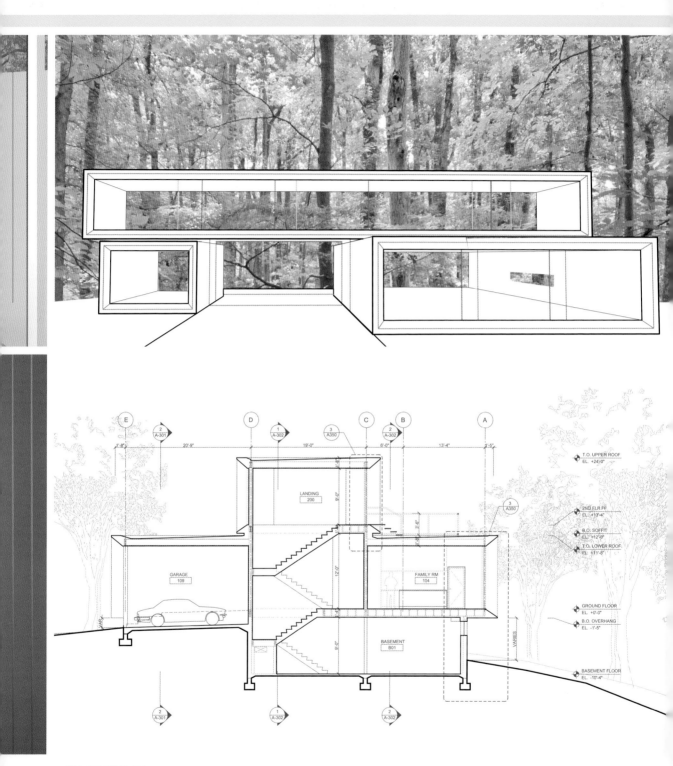

The conceptual see-
through elevation
reflects the project's
intentions as a fram-
ing device for the
landscape.

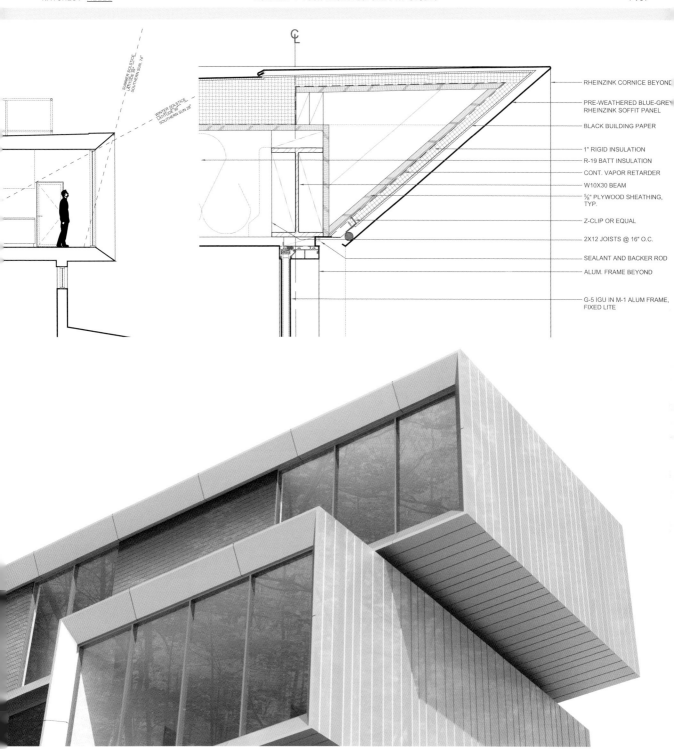

RHEINZINK CORNICE BEYOND

PRE-WEATHERED BLUE-GREY
RHEINZINK SOFFIT PANEL

BLACK BUILDING PAPER

1" RIGID INSULATION

R-19 BATT INSULATION

CONT. VAPOR RETARDER

W10X30 BEAM

⅝" PLYWOOD SHEATHING,
TYP.

Z-CLIP OR EQUAL

2X12 JOISTS @ 16" O.C.

SEALANT AND BACKER ROD

ALUM. FRAME BEYOND

G-5 IGU IN M-1 ALUM FRAME,
FIXED LITE

SUMMER SOLSTICE
LATITUDE 38° SOUTHERN SUN: 74°

WINTER SOLSTICE
LATITUDE 38° SOUTHERN SUN: 28°

The upper volume can-
tilevers to express
its separation from the
lower volumes. The bev-
eled detail creates a
paper-thin edge.

Optimized for the solar
angles of the site, the
beveled exterior edges
allow for low winter
sun to enter the house
while protecting the
house from solar heat
gain in the summer.

The BRIDGE HOUSE
frames and cap-
tures views of its
surrounding wooded
landscape.

FORMATS

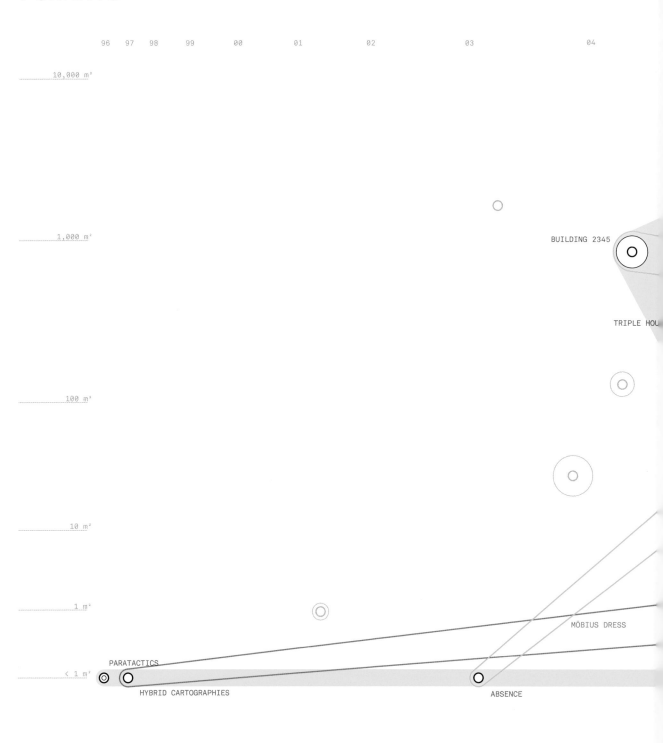

96 97 98 99 00 01 02 03 04

10,000 m²

1,000 m²

BUILDING 2345

TRIPLE HOU

100 m²

10 m²

1 m²

MÖBIUS DRESS

PARATACTICS

< 1 m²

HYBRID CARTOGRAPHIES

ABSENCE

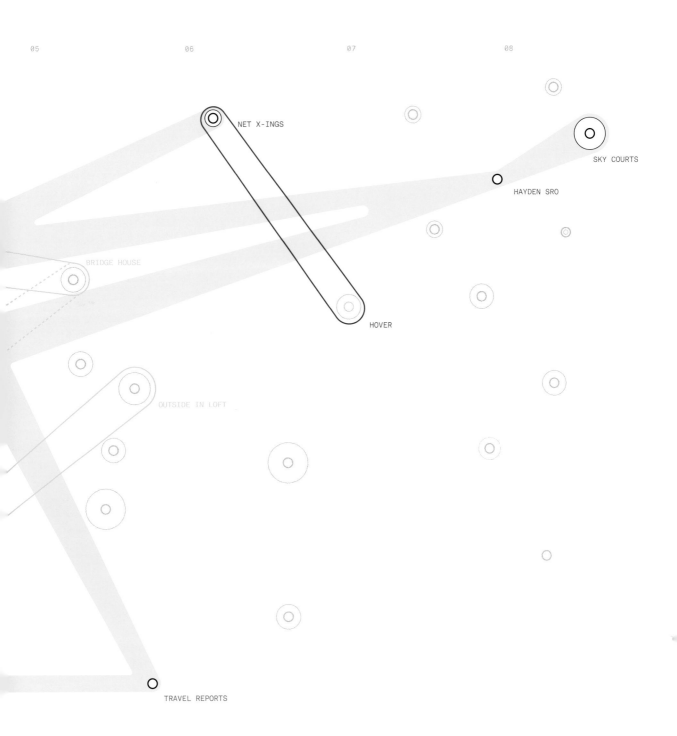

05   06   07   08

NET X-INGS

SKY COURTS

HAYDEN SRO

BRIDGE HOUSE

HOVER

OUTSIDE IN LOFT

TRAVEL REPORTS

Architecture's codes, regulations, norms, and typologies embody much of its hardwired cumulative intelligence. This intelligence structures the discipline, defining its limits and mapping out the "rules of the game"—its basic architectural format. Our focus on format as a research agenda enables us to investigate the role of constraints in architecture while opening up a new realm for formal innovation. Working simultaneously at the scale of the book, the installation, and the building, we are interested in testing strategies that exploit common rules to create uncommon projects, inviting innovation to emerge from within the organizational logic of a project's constraints.

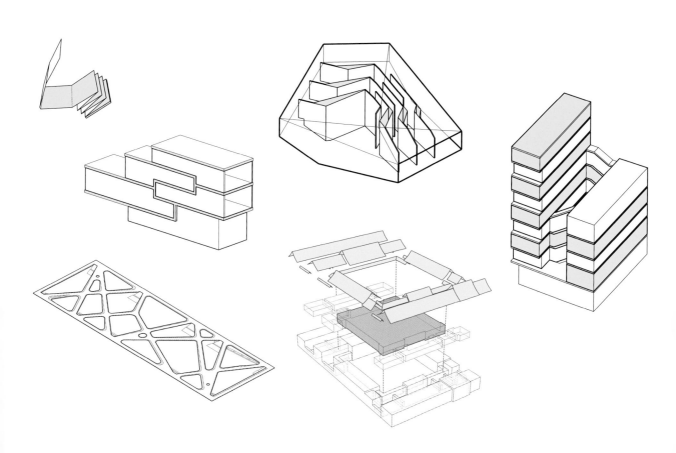

Architecture has long exploited publication as a means of extending a spatial agenda beyond the building site into the realm of mass media. Architects from Vitruvius to Venturi have relied on printed treatises and manifestos for transmission of ideas, recognizing that publication and publicity are integrally linked to architectural projects. Though distinct disciplines, the traditions of the book and the building are complementary and codependent. Their products may appear entirely different, but both book design and architectural design offer opportunities to examine the relationship between form and content.

The four books which introduce this chapter investigate format as a generator of design research. ABSENCE takes the volume of the book as a solid to be excavated, making voids within it. HYBRID CARTOGRAPHIES challenges the idea that a book is linear, providing multiple paths through itself by means of a specific folding technique. PARATACTICS is bound on two sides, displacing the point of entry to the center of the page and engaging the reader in the conscious act of tearing open a book. TRAVEL REPORTS repackages individual booklets into an interlocking container that allows the reader to reorganize the collection of folios. In each case, the reformatted structure of the book responds to both its contents and its constraints. The scale of these books encourages format-based design explorations, allowing them to act as prototypes for larger spatial and architectural concepts.

TRIPLE HOUSE looks like a single-family detached house in a suburban context. This post-nuclear family house, however, is in fact three houses bundled together to give privacy to three generations of a family living under one roof. The combination of five floors of program within a zoning-mandated fifty-foot height limit led to the design of an interlocking section for BUILDING 2345. Each floor has a compressed area of eight-foot-high ceilings in the core zone as well as thirteen-foot ceilings beyond the core. The limits imposed by zoning ordinance produce an organizational solution that transforms a constraint into an amenity.

Bundling and intertwining are also the logics for the HAYDEN SRO, where distinct programs that are spatially similar but socially antithetical—an SRO (single-room occupancy) apartment building and a boutique hotel—are combined in a single building. Limiting points of contact between the two programs within the structure creates physical divisions but maintains visual connections between user groups, reformatting the relationship between habitation and transience. NET X-INGS proposes a pedestrian link over Lake Shore Drive in Chicago that transforms the bridge into a network. The web of connections spanning the roadway creates mutually stabilizing components and offers the pedestrian multiple paths and trajectories.

Building traditions also constitute a distinct cultural format, where configurations and relationships evoke collectively legible cultural meanings. Asked to design a corporate headquarters and villa based on the traditional Chinese courtyard house, we confronted an existing building typology as an architectural format. SKY COURTS I and II reinterpret traditional architectural types into contemporary forms, testing the limits for the reinvention of a typological format.

Engaging format as the generator of design questions the neutral status of the form in format. Format, typology, and tradition are not unmotivated; their forms and conventions reinforce the status quo. By problematizing formats, types, and conventions, we seek to dislodge habits and trigger new methods of design innovation. These projects promote the testing of architecture's structuring limits as a means of reinvigorating it. In doing so, we oscillate back and forth between internal rules, external constraints, programmatic requirements, and design ambitions.

QUATRO LIBRI

Highlighting the relationship between form and content, the following four book projects find innovative ways to structure the book and spatialize its format.

TRAVEL REPORTS compiles the experiences of individual Deborah J. Norden Fund travel grant award recipients. Designed as a compact box set, each individual grantee's research is given a discrete folded leaflet to represent their travel experience. In order to contain their collective experiences, a bifold, double-hinged box houses the individual leaflets. Noted only by longitude and latitude, the loose individual folios may be reordered and recompiled by the reader.

PARATACTICS seeks to engage the reader in the act of reading. Bound on both sides and perforated down the middle, PARATACTICS forces the reader to tear the book along its center line, breaking the book as a first step toward reading it. Once halved, PARATACTICS reveals its organization—text fills one half of the book, images the other. Flipping through the pages, a reader may juxtapose any text with any image, creating an open narrative.

HYBRID CARTOGRAPHIES is both a map and a detour. Juxtaposing three different market typologies, graphics and text narrate a jointly historical, social, and spatial perspective of Seoul with prescribed paths and open trajectories, inviting the reader to engage with the book in a nonlinear manner. Constructed from a single sheet of paper sixty centimeters square, printed on front and back, and folded, the book is also a Möbius loop.

ABSENCE (published by Printed Matter and the Whitney Museum of American Art) is a memorial to the events of September 11, 2001. The absence of the World Trade Center towers is represented in the void cut through 110 of its pages, corresponding to each floor of the twin towers. Made of an ephemeral material, paper, and scaled to the individual, its site is between a pair of hands. ABSENCE explores the use of mass, materiality, and void to communicate its content without any use of text; the void is the content.

The section of TRAVEL REPORTS reveals two sides packed together to create spatial pockets for the leaflets.

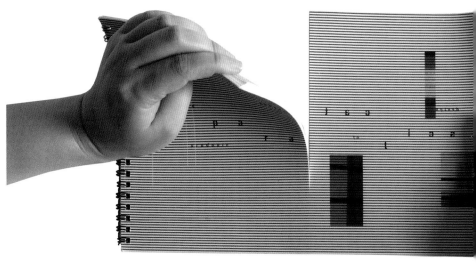

PARATACTICS plays with the concept of a "double bind." Literally doubly bound, this book must be ripped in half in order to be read.

Halved, PARATACTICS juxtaposes one book of text with another of images, allowing the reader to participate in rejoining its content.

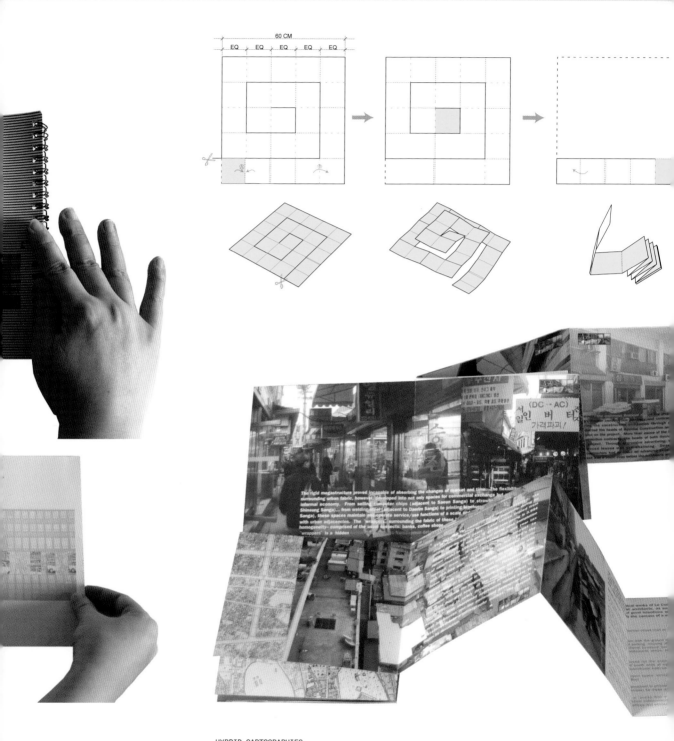

HYBRID CARTOGRAPHIES
begins as a single
sheet. The center of the
front is attached to
the end of the back
along prescribed folds
and cuts, transforming
the single sheet into
a Möbius book.

ABSENCE's mute exterior
conceals its interior
space. It is a negative
scale model with the
plan of the twin towers
cut from 110 pages.

POST-NUCLEAR PACKING

Format implies a codified collection of rules, relationships, and needs. The format of a house, like the format of a book, comes with an embedded litany of assumptions that must be challenged. Housing three generations under one roof, the TRIPLE HOUSE is a post-nuclear family house that reexamines issues of private and public within the suburban house.

The clients for the house are empty nesters whose ambition is to design-build a house that brings the family back together: the parents, their children and their future grandchildren. Balancing the delicate needs of privacy and collectivity within what will appear to be a single-family structure, the house is conceived of as a bundle of distinct private domestic spaces composed within a singular form. The geometry of the house is an articulated manifold: a three-car garage port on the ground floor is its input, and three bedrooms with a view of a ravine are its output. Each car port connects semi-autonomously to the upstairs bedrooms while simultaneously linking to the shared communal spaces.

The post-nuclear house functions within the parameters of the suburban American dream—the architecturally distinct detached dwelling. It is nuanced by a cultural specificity that desires greater intergenerational connectivity while maintaining the needs of convenience, privacy, and territoriality. The TRIPLE HOUSE packages these needs into a compact and multistranded structure, encasing its multiple and semi-independent domestic spaces within the folds of the bundled manifold. The home acts as a series of flows, valves, and ports, allowing the family to inhabit a single house while maintaining distinct use patterns and regulating its mixture of shared domesticity.

Three branches of one family live under the same roof. TRIPLE HOUSE provides a shared common space as well as triply redundant circulation to the private zones on the second floor.

Shared space on the
first floor bifurcates
into private living
quarters above.

The house's massing minimizes the exterior volume while reflecting its interior program, desired site orientation for view, and entry.

Each family has
its own garage,
entrance, and inte-
rior circulation.

A series of study
models shows the
basic formal tactic
used in this proj-
ect: splitting in
plan and section.

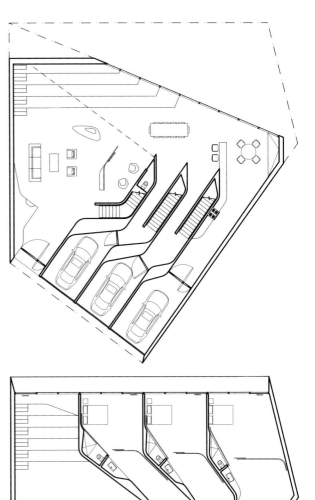

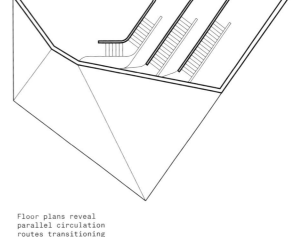

Floor plans reveal
parallel circulation
routes transitioning
from collective ground-
floor public space to
second-floor private
spaces separated by
three sets of private
stairs.

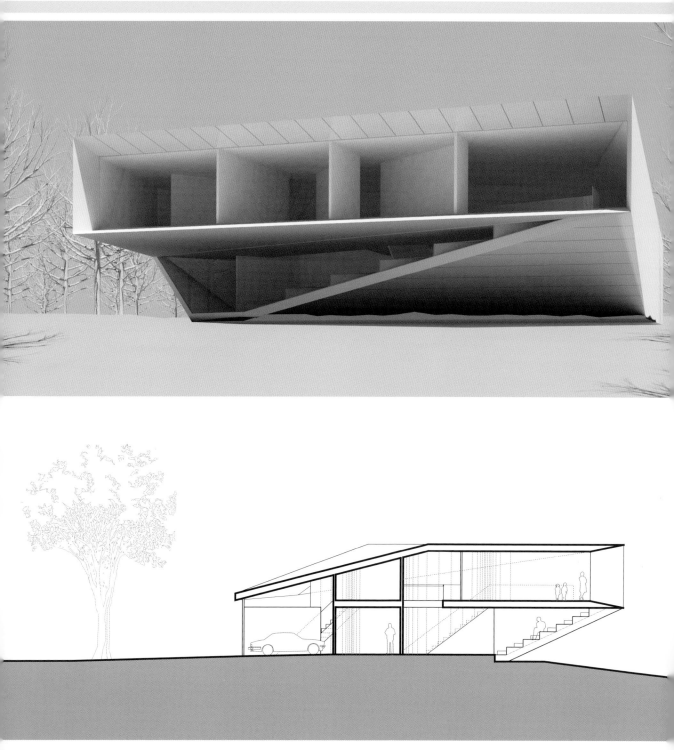

The upper level
of the house
cantilevers toward
the forest view.

The undercut of the cantilever doubles as circulation and seating, creating a collective indoor amphitheater in the house's most shared space.

INTERLOCKED ZONING

Architecture responds to numerous constraints—regulatory, programmatic, structural, material, and logistical. Zoning and other legal restrictions often dictate the shape of the built environment. BUILDING 2345 mines these regulatory constraints for their reformatting potential.

Restrictions to BUILDING 2345's site in southeast Washington DC include a small and narrow lot, a floor area ratio (FAR) of 1.5 with a mixed-use bonus of 1, a height limit of 50 feet, and a 3-part program composed of office, retail, and residential spaces. Five floors of varying dimension based on their respective programs are stacked—shifting alternately toward the building's front and back—and connected at the central service core. With constant floor-to-ceiling heights of eight feet, six inches along the vertical core, each floor expands upward or downward to create variable-height spaces for both living and working.

While the front and back elevations appear to be a three-story building, the interlocking five stories are revealed on the side elevation. Standing-seam metal panels and vertical slot windows fill in the articulated slab profile. BUILDING 2345 maximizes its FAR potential and packs five floors of disparate uses into a tight zoning envelope, discovering unexpected potential in the constraints.

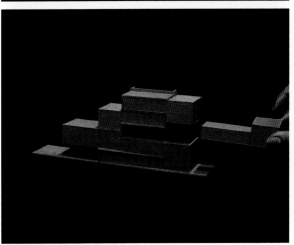

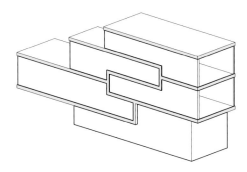

Study models demonstrate how the five floors stack efficiently into the core and interlock with each other.

Front and side facades
present differing
scalar perspectives.
Three stories register
on the front facade,
while five stories can
be read from the side
elevation.

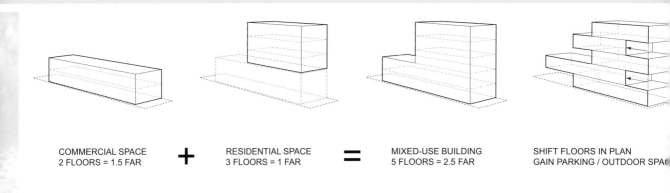

COMMERCIAL SPACE
2 FLOORS = 1.5 FAR

+

RESIDENTIAL SPACE
3 FLOORS = 1 FAR

=

MIXED-USE BUILDING
5 FLOORS = 2.5 FAR

SHIFT FLOORS IN PLAN
GAIN PARKING / OUTDOOR SPACE

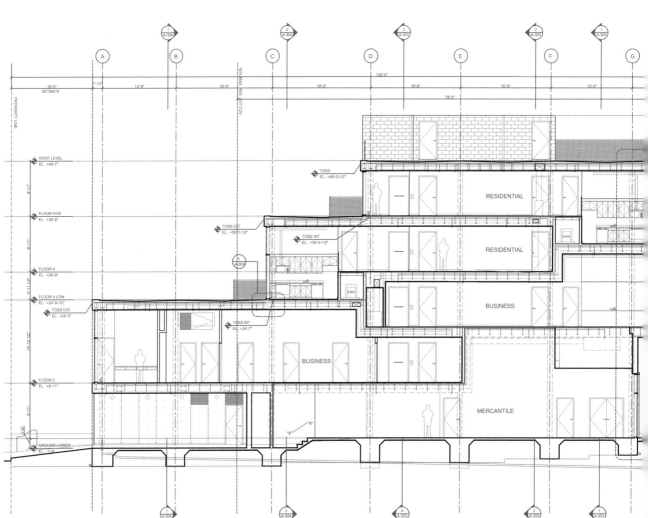

Massing diagrams
trace zoning regu-
lations and volume
modifications.

The building's section
reveals the relation-
ships among the mixed
residential, office, and
commercial programs.

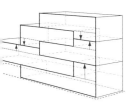

HIFT FLOORS IN SECTION
REATE DOUBLE HEIGHT
TERIOR SPACES

NORTH - SOUTH
= 1'-0"

Each program piece
stacks efficiently in
section at the core, and
expands at the front or
back to create a taller
ceiling height.

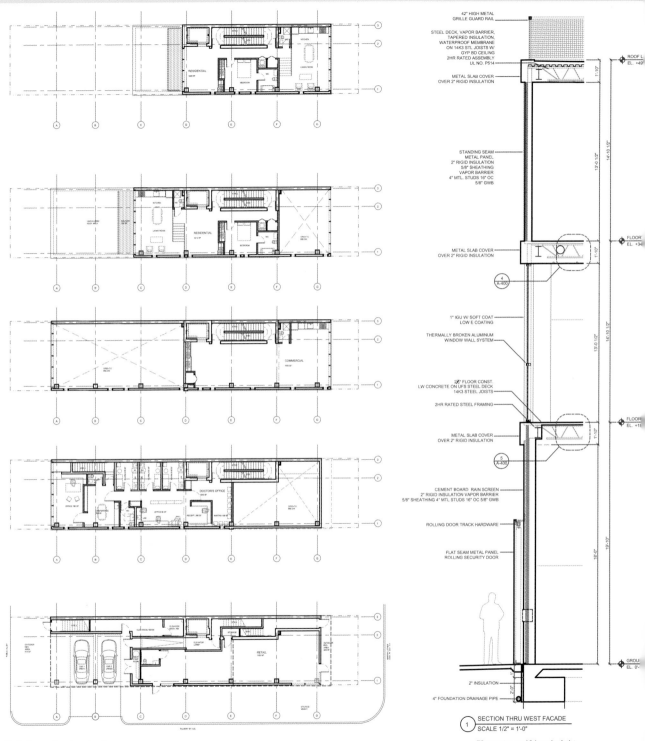

Each floor plan is sized to accommodate its program, resulting in the square-footage variations of each floor.

Floor-to-ceiling-height glass on the front and back facades provides views to the open interior spaces.

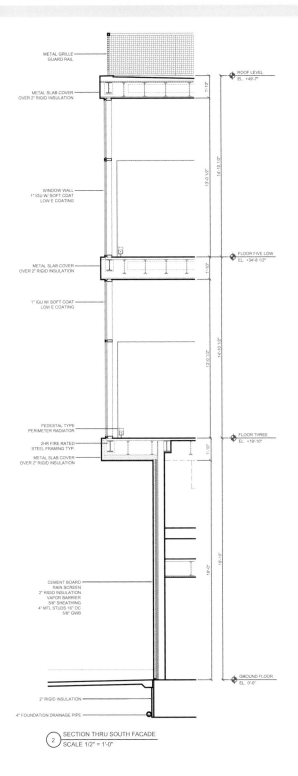

METAL GRILLE
GUARD RAIL

ROOF LEVEL
EL. +49'-7"

METAL SLAB COVER
OVER 2" RIGID INSULATION

WINDOW WALL
1" IGU W/ SOFT COAT
LOW E COATING

FLOOR FIVE LOW
EL. +34'-8 1/2"

METAL SLAB COVER
OVER 2" RIGID INSULATION

1" IGU W/ SOFT COAT
LOW E COATING

PEDESTAL TYPE
PERIMETER RADIATOR

FLOOR THREE
EL. +19'-10"

2HR FIRE RATED
STEEL FRAMING TYP.

METAL SLAB COVER
OVER 2" RIGID INSULATION

CEMENT BOARD
RAIN SCREEN
2" RIGID INSULATION
VAPOR BARRIER
5/8" SHEATHING
4" MTL STUDS 16" OC
5/8" GWB

GROUND FLOOR
EL. 0'-0"

2" RIGID INSULATION

4" FOUNDATION DRAINAGE PIPE

2 SECTION THRU SOUTH FACADE
   SCALE 1/2" = 1'-0"

The floor slabs are
articulated on the
facade with metal
panels and glass set
in from the face of
the articulated slab.

DOUBLE HELIX

Investigation of formats of varying scales illuminates unexpected affinities and relationships, challenging assumptions that drive conventions of form in format. HAYDEN SRO proposes a pair of unlikely but dimensionally equivalent programs—the boutique hotel and single-room occupancy housing (SRO). Identifying and exploiting the spatial and infrastructural similarities between the two programs suggests ways to both capitalize on and accommodate their combination.

The Hayden Building in Boston, designed in 1875 by H. H. Richardson, fills a footprint far too small to accommodate current commercial uses. Combining this site with an adjacent parcel produces an opportunity for adaptive reuse with SRO housing. Despite sharing a history of transient occupancy as well as an identical floor layout, SRO and boutique hotel programs are an unlikely pair, as their respective clienteles are assumed to be incompatible.

HAYDEN SRO subtly probes this assumption by intertwining both programs. Organized in a helical fashion around a shared vertical courtyard, units of each type are connected by independent circulation systems. Limited points of contact between the two programs within the structure maintain de facto divisions between user groups, resulting in a reformatted study of inhabitation and transience.

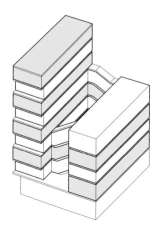

On the compact urban site, floors stack and interlock to accommodate the varying programs.

The HAYDEN SRO inter-
twines the adaptive
reuse of the historic
Hayden Building with a
new structure to accom-
modate both a boutique
hotel and SRO housing.

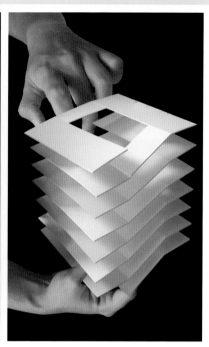

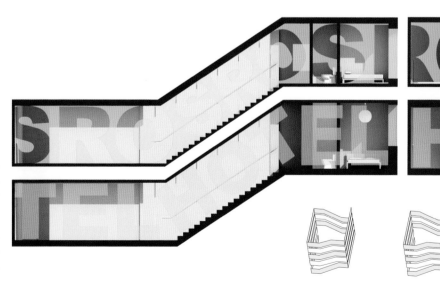

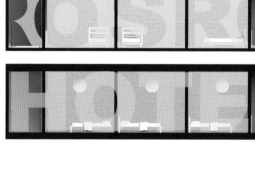

Color-coded study models demonstrate the intertwined circulation of the hotel and SRO programs.

A double-helical circulation path allows the SRO and hotel to have completely independent and continuous circulation.

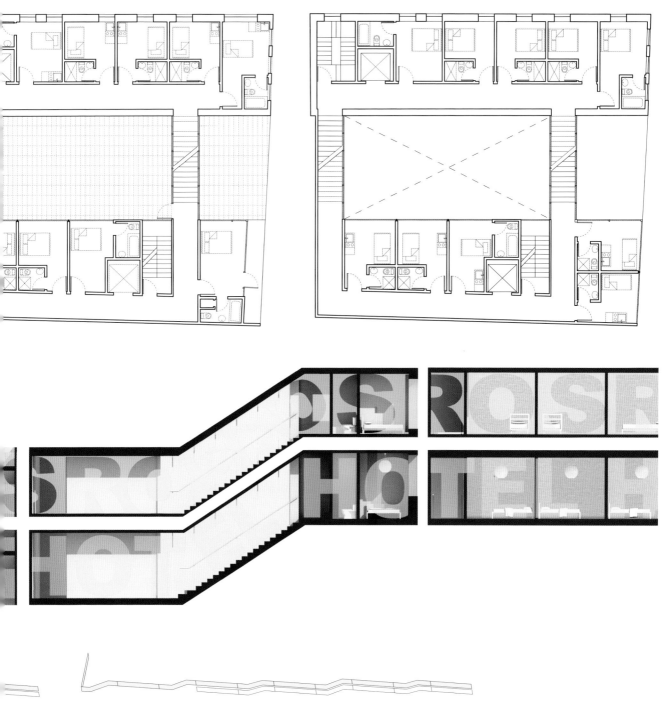

The plan calls for
circulation to run along
the parti-wall edge
of each bar building,
preventing room-to-
room views across the
courtyard.

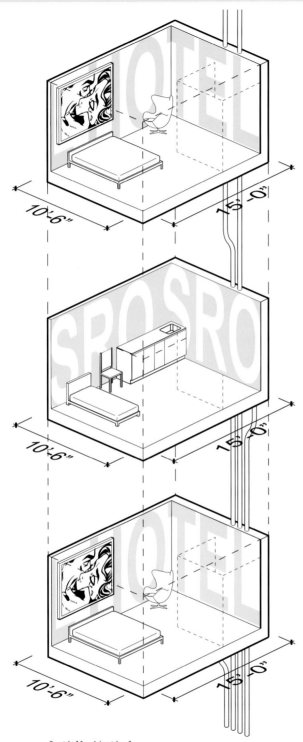

10'-6"

15'-0"

10'-6"

15'-0"

10'-6"

15'-0"

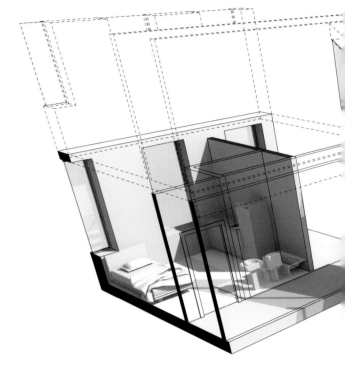

Spatially identical,
the two programs are
differentiated only
by their contents,
as required by each
user group.

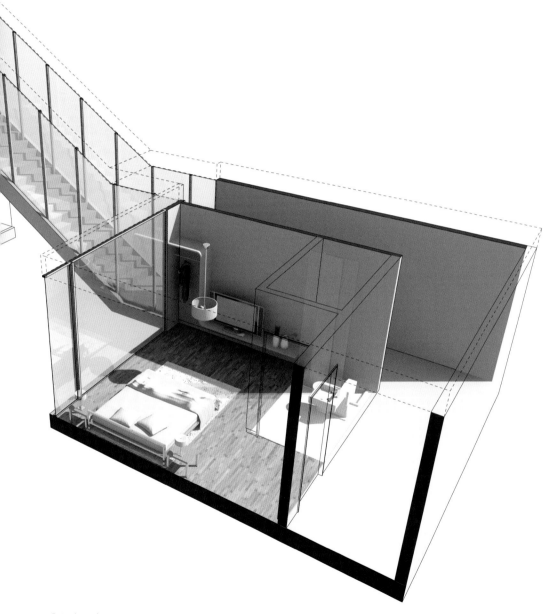

Interior views
illuminate the
identical spatial
needs of each
program type.

MULTIPLE SPANS

Responding to the monumentality of Daniel Burnham's Grant Park and the horizontality of Lake Michigan's waterfront, NET X-INGS connects the two with a network strategy. The "net" is the geometric intermediary between the line and the plane. While the park and fountain are monumental, hierarchical, and singular, NET X-INGS is horizontal, lateral, and multiple, creating numerous opportunities to cross, view, and hover above the city.

The bridge consists of a series of stressed-ribbon tension structures that span Chicago's Lake Shore Drive between concrete piers. Bearing cables are strung across the road and act as support for hung precast-concrete panels. The multiple spans provide structural stability by laterally bracing each other. The massive concrete piers support the bridge, resisting the large horizontal forces produced by the cables while forming the stairway access.

The bridge profile tapers to emphasize the thinness of the bridge section, alternately beveled up and down. The upward-facing bevel is lined with photovoltaic cells and the edges of the bridge are lined with light-emitting diode strips. The light direction differs in alternate areas, pointing up for the pedestrians and pointing down for the motorists. NET X-INGS is not simply a connector, but a destination—a place between the park and the waterfront.

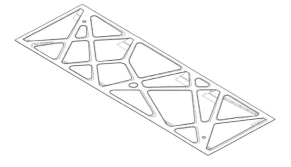

5.

6A.

[5] A SINGLE CABLE LACKS TRANSVERSE STIFFNESS AND CAN SWAY SIDE TO SIDE.

[6] ADDING OPPOSING CABLES PROVIDES BOTH TRANSVERSE STIFFNESS AND ADDITIONAL PATHWAYS [A+B].

The multiple bridges create an elevated pedestrian landscape which hovers above the vehicular traffic.

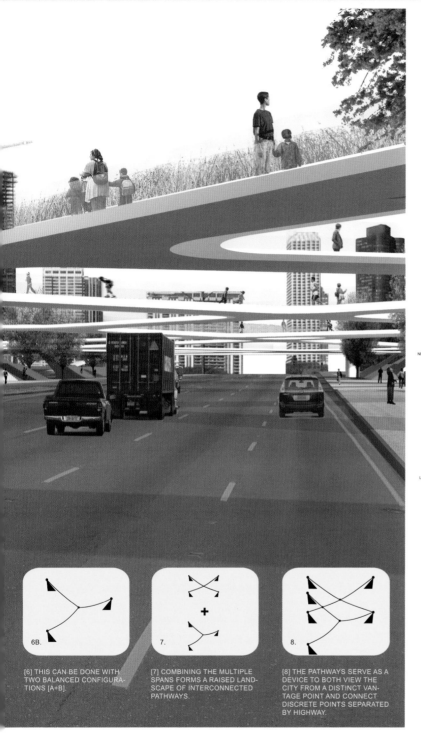

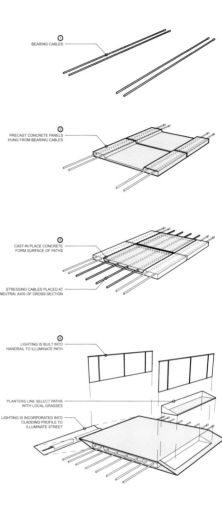

① BEARING CABLES

② PRECAST CONCRETE PANELS
HUNG FROM BEARING CABLES

③ CAST-IN PLACE CONCRETE
FORM SURFACE OF PATHS

STRESSING CABLES PLACED AT
NEUTRAL AXIS OF CROSS-SECTION

④ LIGHTING IS BUILT INTO
HANDRAIL TO ILLUMINATE PATH

PLANTERS LINE SELECT PATHS
WITH LOCAL GRASSES

LIGHTING IS INCORPORATED INTO
CLADDING PROFILE TO
ILLUMINATE STREET

6B.

7.

8.

[6] THIS CAN BE DONE WITH
TWO BALANCED CONFIGURA-
TIONS [A+B].

[7] COMBINING THE MULTIPLE
SPANS FORMS A RAISED LAND-
SCAPE OF INTERCONNECTED
PATHWAYS.

[8] THE PATHWAYS SERVE AS A
DEVICE TO BOTH VIEW THE
CITY FROM A DISTINCT VAN-
TAGE POINT AND CONNECT
DISCRETE POINTS SEPARATED
BY HIGHWAY.

Pretensioned cables
run through cast-
concrete decking that
supports the surface.

PARALLEL PROCESS

Diverse factors—physical, pragmatic, cultural, and historical—inform typology. Unlike physical and pragmatic constraints, whose underlying rules and logics are easily unpacked, cultural and historical forces are harder to unravel. Typologies are often embedded in years of collective architectural research and practice. Asked to reinterpret the Chinese courtyard typology as a modern corporate clubhouse, these two projects use their constraints—the building typology and a mandate for sloped roofs—as opportunities to transform this traditional building type into a contemporary architectural proposition for a modern mixed-use program.

Two proposals for SKY COURTS designed in parallel explore these constraints as opportunities to rethink the form of the corporate clubhouse in two different ways. Both incorporate short-term housing, office space, and entertainment facilities, but vary in their usage of the logics of the courtyard and sloped roof. SCHEME 1 has a system of slopes in plan and section that join or split to create varying courtyards and accommodate different programs. By systematizing the bent program strips, the project creates a compact landscape of peaks and valleys. SCHEME 2 packs many courtyards into a defined perimeter and utilizes the sloped roof to accommodate program in the wedge between courtyards, allowing the project to read as 100 percent courtyard from above. The traditional courtyard typology is distorted to accommodate the site and the variety of program elements.

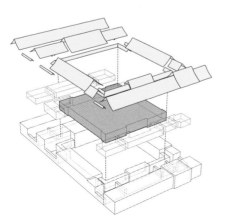

SCHEME 1, top, utilizes slopes in plan and section to compose a constructed landscape. SCHEME 2, bottom, packs the courtyards to create an introverted organizational logic.

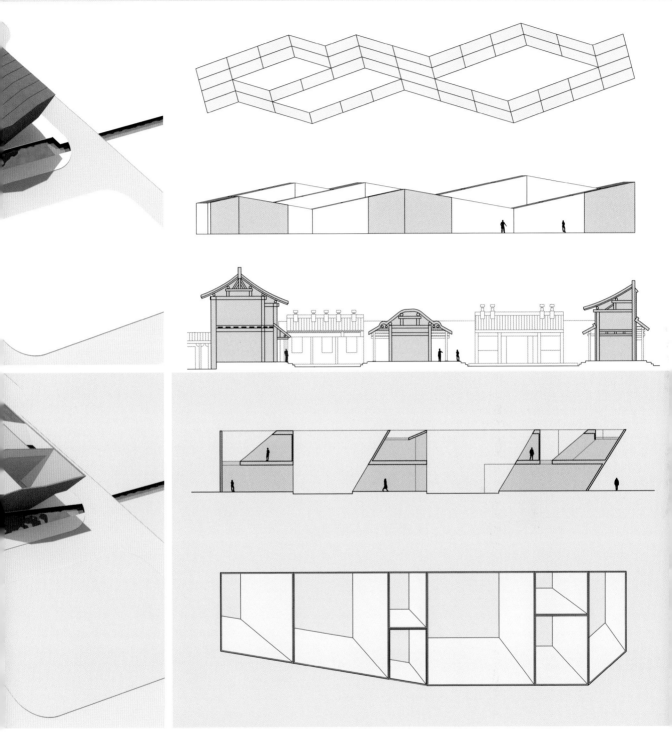

Each scheme interprets
the traditional court-
yard form, shown sec-
tionally, above center.

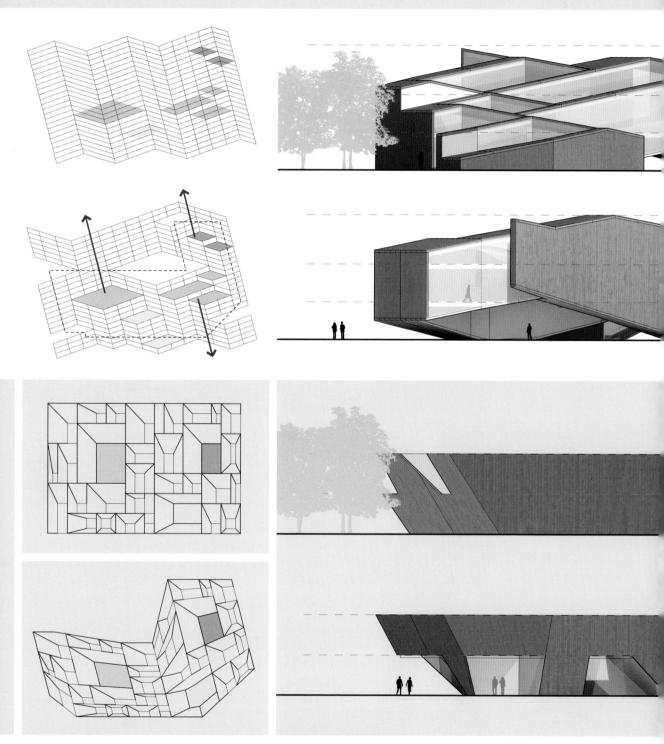

Each scheme enables
the clustering of
specific internal
programmatic zones.

Three primary programmed
courtyards for live,
work, and play organize
each scheme. The geom-
etries deform to accom-
modate the shape and
setbacks of the site.

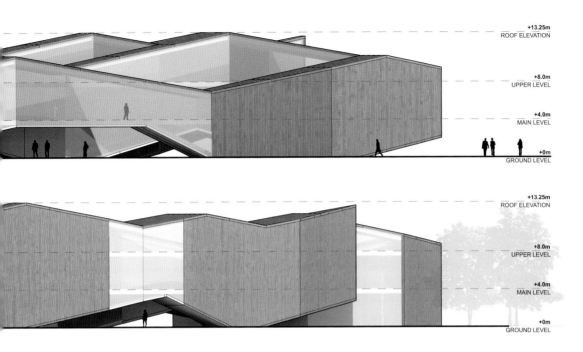

The elevations of each
scheme reflect the
different natures of
the courtyard logics
on the exterior of
the buildings.

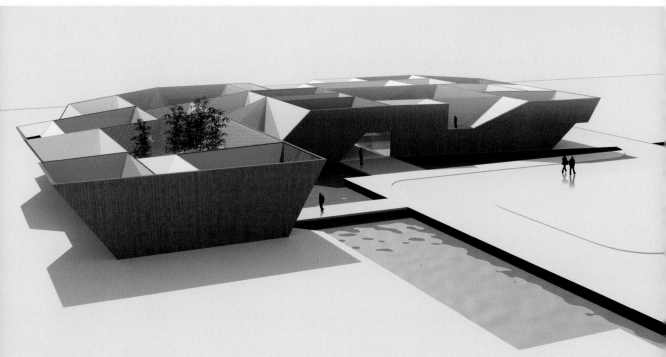

Each scheme engages
the site, pulling
visitors in and
through its network
of courtyards.

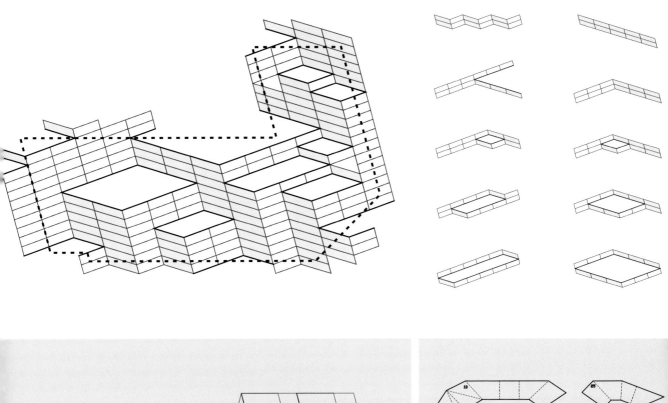

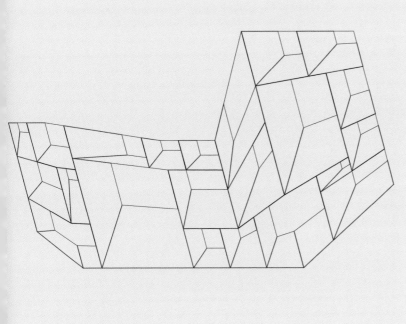

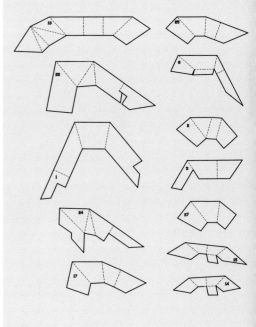

Unfolded surface pat-
terns demonstrate each
scheme's generative
logic. SCHEME 1 splits
and folds strips while
SCHEME 2 packs cellular
volumes.

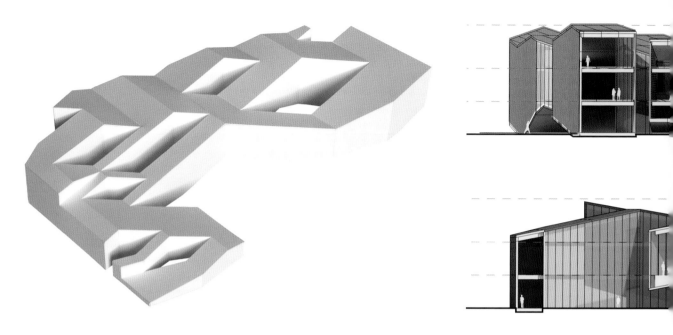

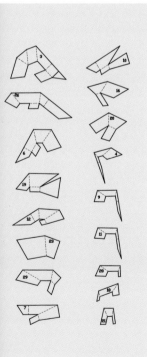

Sections reveal the
internal organizational
logic of the banded and
packed schemes.

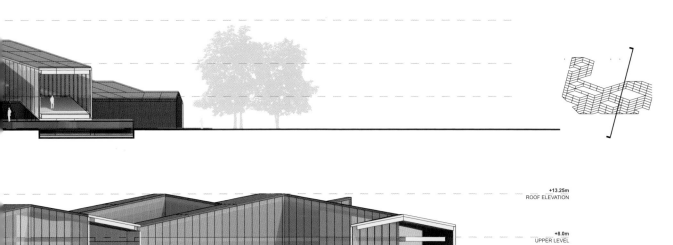

+13.25m
ROOF ELEVATION

+8.0m
UPPER LEVEL

+4.0m
MAIN LEVEL

+0m
GROUND LEVEL

+8.0m
ROOF LEVEL

+4.0m
MAIN LEVEL

+0m
GROUND LEVEL

+8.0m
ROOF LEVEL

+4.0m
MAIN LEVEL

+0m
GROUND LEVEL

Courtyard views dem-
onstrate the complex
spatial and volu-
metric qualities of
each scheme.

SCHEME 2's courtyards,
above, invert the
pitched-roof format and
register points of entry
into the complex on the
exterior facades.

SCHEME 1's roof-
scape creates a
collapsed perspec-
tival landscape.

INTERACTIONS

10,000 m²

1,000 m²

100 m²

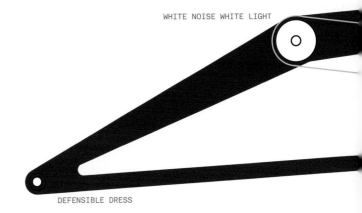

WHITE NOISE WHITE LIGHT

10 m²

1 m²

DEFENSIBLE DRESS

< 1 m²

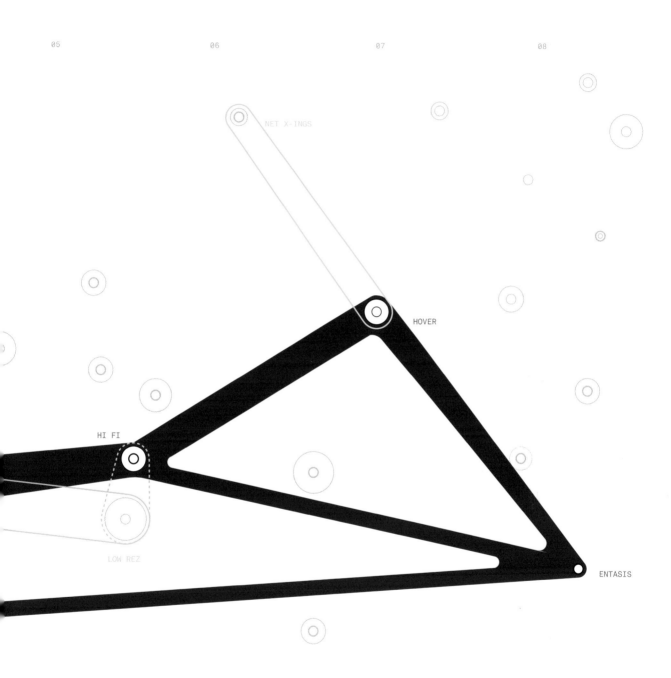

The figure of the cyborg promises the simultaneity of difference: of man and machine, biology and technology, natural and artificial. Incorporated into a single body, this productive hybrid reframes technology in relation to the human body and its environment. The cyborg is the new contemporary archetype, altering existing ecologies by overlaying new sets of relationships between organism and environment. Despite the unprecedented proliferation of ubiquitous computing in daily life, "smartness" in architecture eludes the synthetic promise of the cyborg.

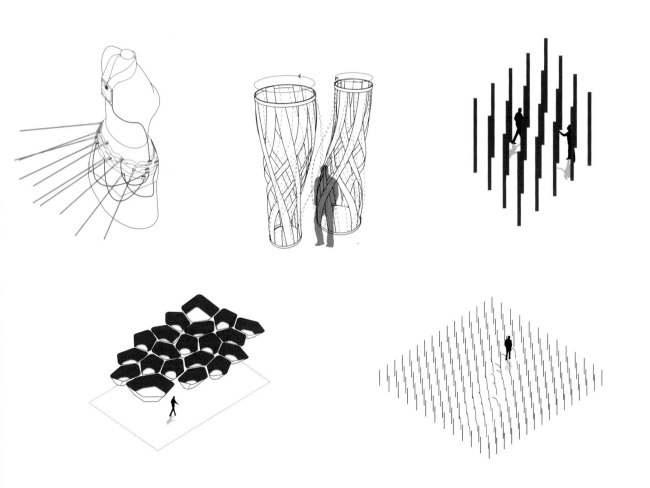

Electronic devices have augmented our built environment for decades. Inserted in and applied to architecture, these discrete machines act like smart parasites on dense hosts. Absorbed into the colloquial vocabulary of the built environment—activating automatic doors, flushing toilets, and regulating temperature in the service of convenience and hygiene—these sensors have brought surveillance, automation, and control into our spaces. At the same time, they have created new opportunities for public engagement, responsiveness, and interaction.

Between the technophilic and technophobic exists a critical terrain created by the intersection of technology, the body, and the built environment.[1] Although architecture habitually incorporates new technological developments while developing technologies of its own, specific electronic advances have recently reframed the potential of responsive environments. Increasingly accessible and customizable devices—including microcontrollers, passive infrared (PIR) sensors, and radio-frequency identification (RFID) tags—are enabling a tighter integration between architecture and electronics, allowing for unusual juxtapositions and hybridization.

Deploying known and emerging technologies in an integral rather than an applied way, the following series of design probes advance an agenda of architecturally enabled public engagement. At the scale of the body, the DEFENSIBLE DRESS delineates an intimate territory of "personal space" through the use of the thermally responsive material nitinol, a shape-memory alloy. At the scale of a room, or in the space between two bodies, ENTASIS creates a dynamic "portal" for the interaction of bodies in space with a kinetic threshold. HI FI develops a volumetric, responsive environment—a cube of space defined by sound and activated by touch. HOVER creates a luminous off-grid canopy that harvests solar energy and transforms it into light to host an array of public activities. Using a custom microcontroller, flexible photovoltaic cells, and a rechargeable battery, the canopy gathers energy during the day and transforms it into lighting at night. The project's production and consumption of energy serve as a way of increasing awareness of the energy crisis and promoting debate and discussion around sustainable energy practices. WHITE NOISE WHITE LIGHT, a field of chest-high fiber-optic stalks and responsive sound, creates an open condition for interactive play. Multiplying a singular indexical response across a field, the project creates an immersive environment that modulates light and sound.

The projects in this chapter investigate participatory environments, responsive architectures, and performative public spaces that combine architecture, technology, and landscape to propose new modes of publicness in the contemporary city. New and unexpected relationships between users and space emerge from the introduction of responsive and interactive environments into the public realm. Temporary or permanent, these techno-architectural interventions become mediating devices between the user, the artifact, and the site. They reposition the body and its relationships using a range of materials—light-emitting diodes (LEDs), photovoltaic cells, and fiber optics—allowing the public to participate in the creation and manipulation of light, sound, movement, and energy. It is through the actions of the public that these projects transform from merely responsive to interactive and adaptive.

Acknowledging the unpredictability of use and experience within architecture, these projects capitalize on the public realm as a fertile testing ground for interactivity, explicitly relying on public participation and play for completion. As testing mechanisms for scripted and unscripted behaviors, these projects are open source. A new form of authorship, open source invites multiple authors to collaborate in the construction of a new artifact: software, encyclopedia content, publication, or environment. Interactive environments provoke an engagement, inviting multiple publics to enter into an open-ended and evolving scenario. The public's participation incorporates its unscripted behavior into the project, relying on the interaction between the two to produce open source architecture.

1. The territory between the technophilic and technophobic has been mapped out by Diller + Scofidio in multiple projects that investigate our ambivalence toward technologies. See Elizabeth Diller and Ricardo Scofidio, Flesh: Architectural Probes (New York: Princeton Architectural Press, 1994).

INCORPORATING BOUNDARIES

At the scale of the body, social norms and personal comfort define an unmarked but generally understood perimeter condition that we maintain as our personal space. A culturally, socially, and individually determined boundary, personal space is constantly calibrated, pushing back against external pressures of public life.

The DEFENSIBLE DRESS project articulates this notion of space as an intimate environment of the body. The dress employs passive infrared (PIR) sensors, a microcontroller, and a series of actuated quills to define a personal-space territory around the body. When the sensor detects the presence of another individual within the user-defined personal-space zone, a calibrated electric current is sent to the quills. Each quill consists of a hollow copper tube that houses a shape-memory alloy nitinol wire in an extreme-temperature polyimide sleeve. When an electronic current runs through the wire, heat causes the alloy to contract. This thermally induced contraction enables the quills to lift and, as the wire cools, slowly release.

The wearer of the dress can customize his or her personal-space threshold by numerically defining their comfort zone. The dress invites the wearer into a changing dialogue with his or her context, in which the dynamic envelope of moving quills manifests the contested zone between personal and public territories. By operating at a scale much smaller than the traditional scale of architecture, the DEFENSIBLE DRESS is portable, customizable, and personal in a very literal way. The garment is a spatial instrument for defining one's private territory as it is encroached upon in the public realm.

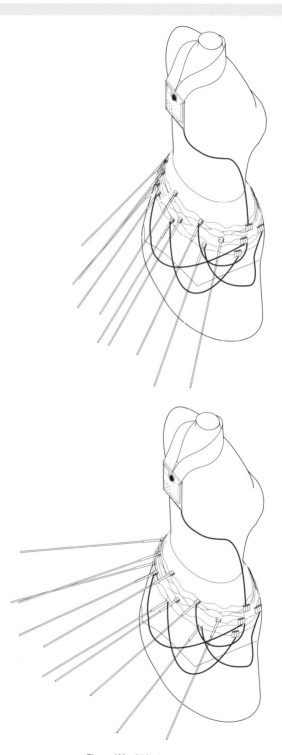

The quills lift to protect and define the wearer's personal space when the PIR sensor registers the approaching presence of another body.

CROWD DYNAMICS

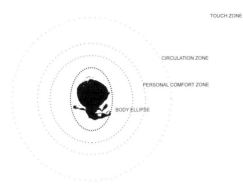

TOUCH ZONE

CIRCULATION ZONE

PERSONAL COMFORT ZONE

BODY ELLIPSE

FRUIN DATA

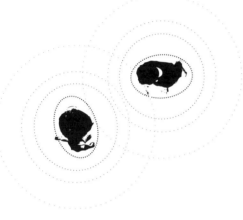

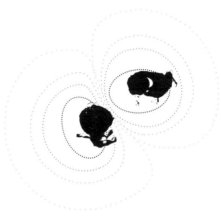

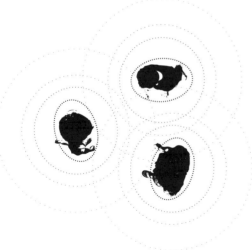

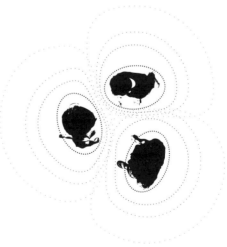

These diagrams of proxemics—
the measurable distance between
people as they interact—use
data on pedestrian planning
from Dr. John J. Fruin to
represent crowd dynamics and
thresholds for personal space
based on social contexts.

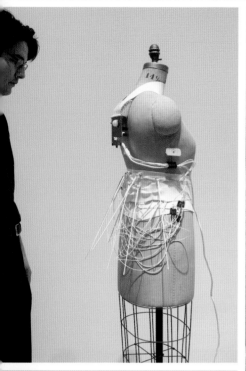

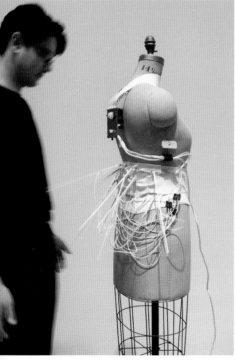

As others violate
the wearer's per-
sonal space, they are
pushed back by the
action of the quills.

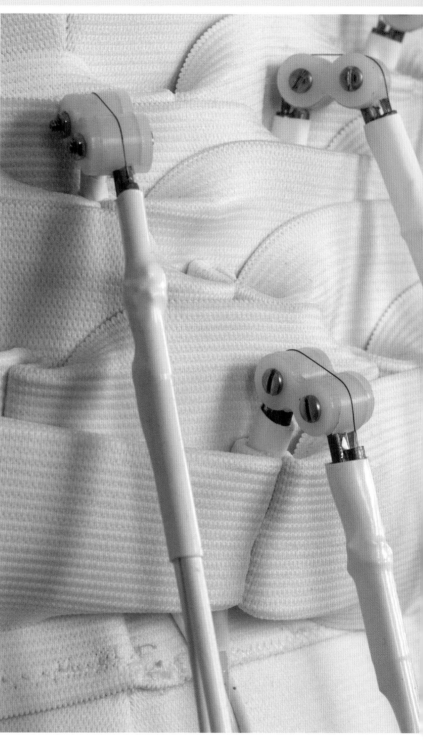

The nitinol wire is housed
in a protective polyimide
tube. Connected to the far
end of the copper tube,
the contracting wire levers
and lifts the quills.

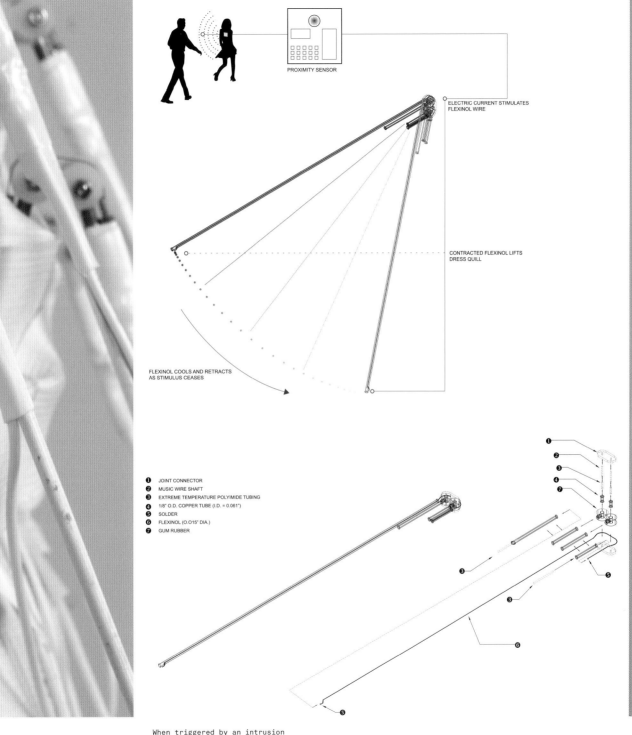

PROXIMITY SENSOR

ELECTRIC CURRENT STIMULATES
FLEXINOL WIRE

CONTRACTED FLEXINOL LIFTS
DRESS QUILL

FLEXINOL COOLS AND RETRACTS
AS STIMULUS CEASES

❶ JOINT CONNECTOR
❷ MUSIC WIRE SHAFT
❸ EXTREME TEMPERATURE POLYIMIDE TUBING
❹ 1/8" O.D. COPPER TUBE (I.D. = 0.061")
❺ SOLDER
❻ FLEXINOL (0.015" DIA.)
❼ GUM RUBBER

When triggered by an intrusion
to the wearer's personal space
by the subsequent electric
current, the nitinol wires
contract suddenly in response
to heat. As they cool, they
slowly return to their original position.

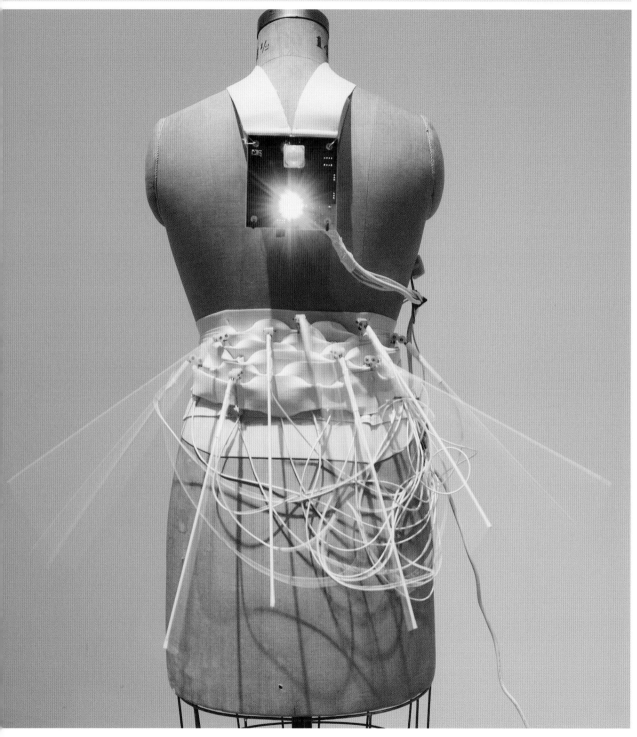

The PIR sensor is worn
separately from the
bustle of quills. The
LEDs on the microcon-
troller illuminate to
register activation by
another body.

BODY CONTORTIONS

Within the tradition of classical architecture, entasis appears as an aberration, contaminating pure mathematics and rectilinearity for the presumably compensatory purpose of perspectival correction. Entasis dynamically expresses a column's load: the swelling in a column's midsection transforms its function into theater. Entasis images tectonics—or rather, a tectonic effect.

As a kinetic sculptural form, ENTASIS amplifies the theatrical potential of this classical principle by assuming a constant state of transformation. This kinetic installation creates an evolving threshold between a pair of nested figures that engage in a "call-and-response" relationship, each transforming from concave to convex and back. Acting as a spatial valve, the piece cycles through related spectrums: closed to open, opaque to transparent, solid to diffuse.

Fabricated from CNC-cut polypropylene, ENTASIS is a materially driven formal device; like its namesake, it reifies its own tectonic order. The flexibility of the material and the structure's computer-controlled rotations produce a syntax of choreographed behaviors. The digitally generated, unrolled, and patterned forms rely on their material properties to calculate the limits of their deformation and govern their behavior, underscoring the "form" in perform.

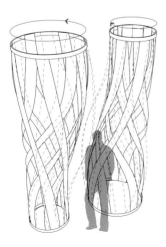

Small scale models of ENTASIS study the movement of the woven columns in response to rotation, torque, and compression, testing their relationship and the threshold between them.

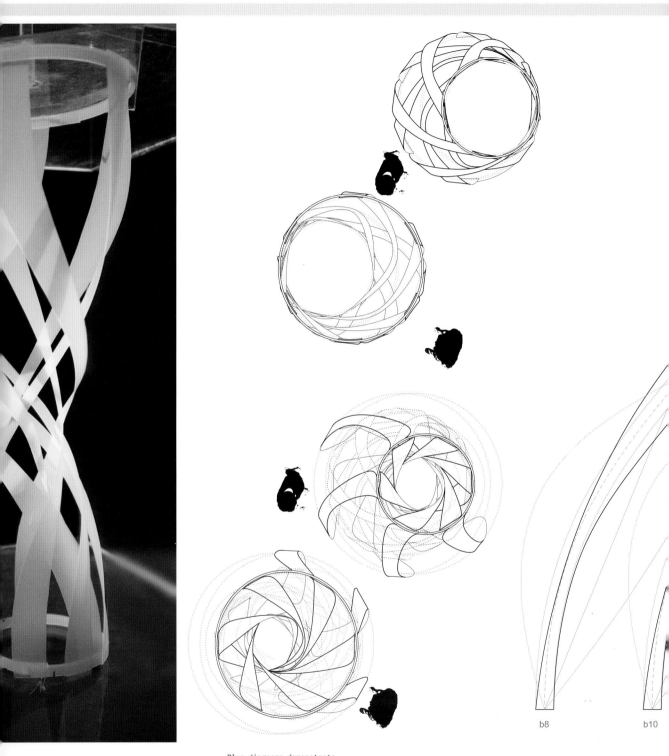

Plan diagrams demonstrate
the relationship between the
rotation of the top of the
columns, the expansion in
their midsections, and the
transformation of the space
between them.

b8   b10

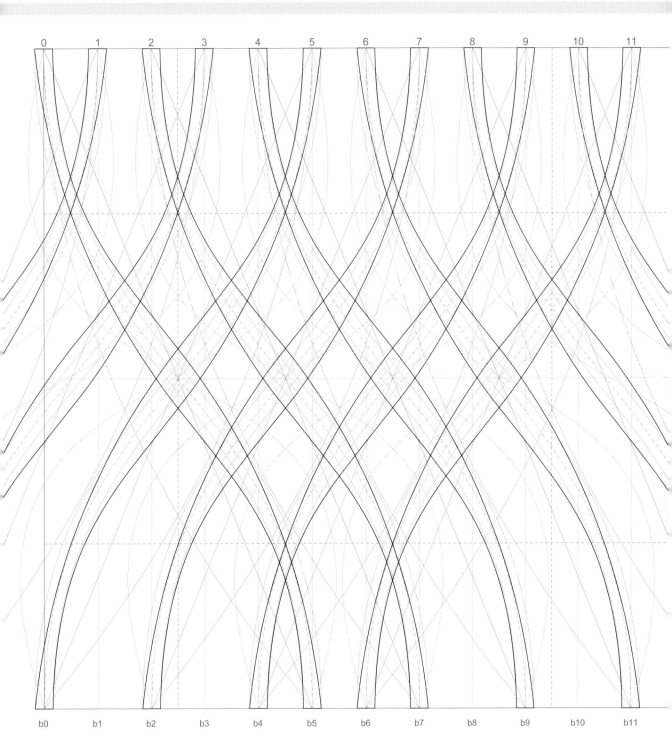

0   1   2   3   4   5   6   7   8   9   10   11

b0   b1   b2   b3   b4   b5   b6   b7   b8   b9   b10   b11

Two-dimensional drawings
of the unrolled column
bands reflect the regula-
ting lines for the
spline geometry of the
woven column.

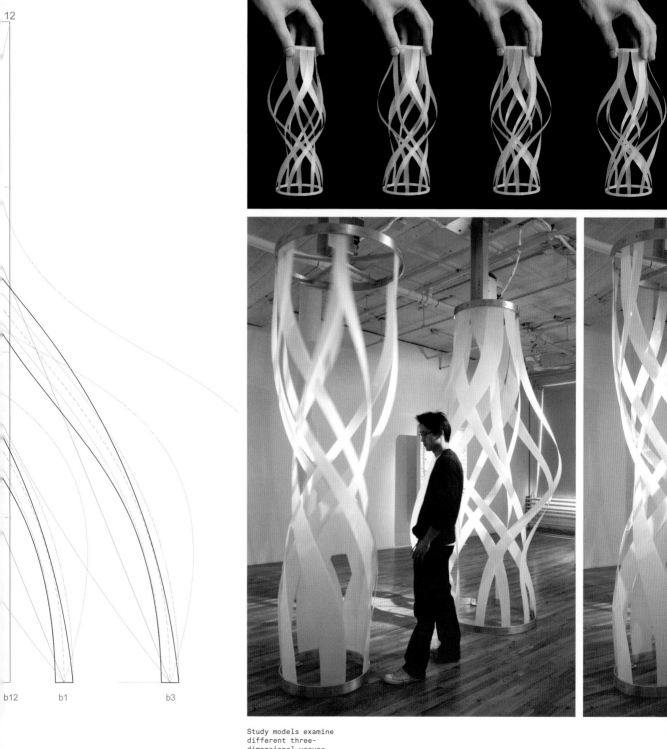

b12   b1   b3

Study models examine
different three-
dimensional weaves
and the effect of
rotation on the vari-
ous weave patterns
as the column twists.

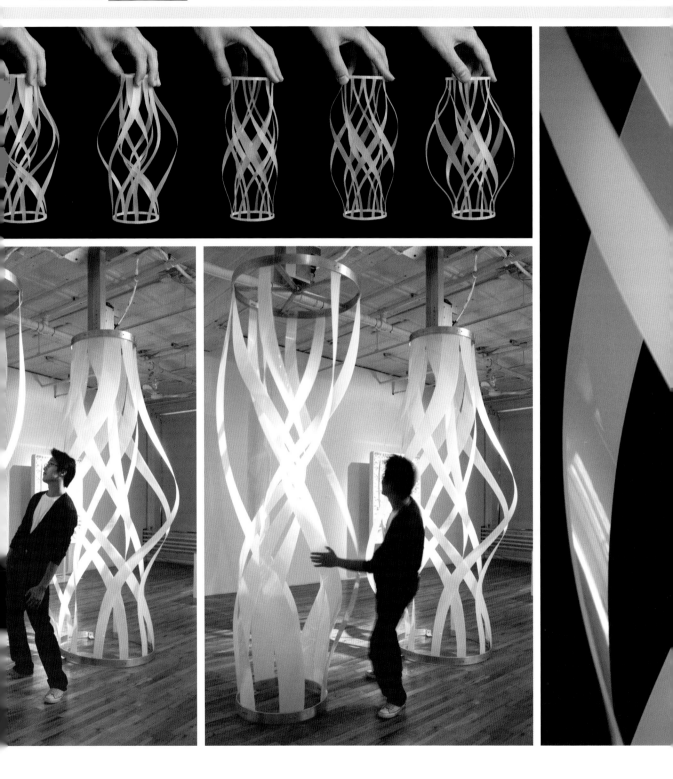

TOUCH SENSITIVE

HI FI invites the public into an interactive sculptural field of play. Designed as a public, architecturally scaled musical instrument, the project occupies a portion of the wide Vermont Avenue sidewalk in Washington DC with a grid of twenty touch-activated sound poles. The dense grouping of thin columns inserts itself into the stream of everyday urban circulation, inviting pedestrians into a field of play with its own parameters and rules for inhabitation and performance.

The rules of HI FI are embedded in its grid of sound- and light-emitting stainless steel poles. The poles, scaled to the human body, are spaced an arm's length apart. The body, a natural electric conductor, triggers the metal pole to emit a sound by changing its capacitance. All the poles are operated and triggered independently but also networked together, allowing a single touch on one pole to trigger a series of related sounds elsewhere in the grove.

Each of the unique sound samples were designed to have a simple repetitive or logarithmic structure. However, when the individual sound samples are overlaid within the field by multiple participants, they create a complex layering of continuously evolving composition. Using the human touch to create a responsive environment of soft sonic envelopes, the public activates the field and engages in play and performance.

The prototype is made from flat sheets of quarter-inch-thick polypropylene. The translucent quality of the material transmits light through the layers of woven bands.

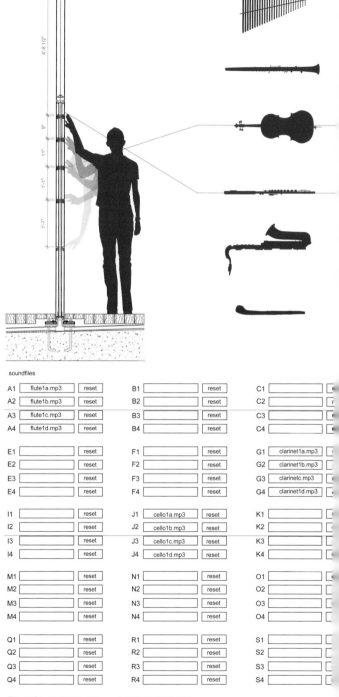

soundfiles

A1	flute1a.mp3	reset	B1		reset	C1		
A2	flute1b.mp3	reset	B2		reset	C2		
A3	flute1c.mp3	reset	B3		reset	C3		
A4	flute1d.mp3	reset	B4		reset	C4		
E1		reset	F1		reset	G1	clarinet1a.mp3	
E2		reset	F2		reset	G2	clarinet1b.mp3	
E3		reset	F3		reset	G3	clarinetc.mp3	
E4		reset	F4		reset	G4	clarinet1d.mp3	
I1		reset	J1	cello1a.mp3	reset	K1		
I2		reset	J2	cello1b.mp3	reset	K2		
I3		reset	J3	cello1c.mp3	reset	K3		
I4		reset	J4	cello1d.mp3	reset	K4		
M1		reset	N1		reset	O1		
M2		reset	N2		reset	O2		
M3		reset	N3		reset	O3		
M4		reset	N4		reset	O4		
Q1		reset	R1		reset	S1		
Q2		reset	R2		reset	S2		
Q3		reset	R3		reset	S3		
Q4		reset	R4		reset	S4		

Twenty custom-fabricated poles are arrayed in a grid spaced by the human reach, allowing partici-pants to touch multiple poles simultaneously.

The pole segments are calibrated to the scale of the human body so that the average person can reach all four active segments of the pole.

A custom-designed tool maps sounds to pole segments in order to test the layered effect of various sound samples.

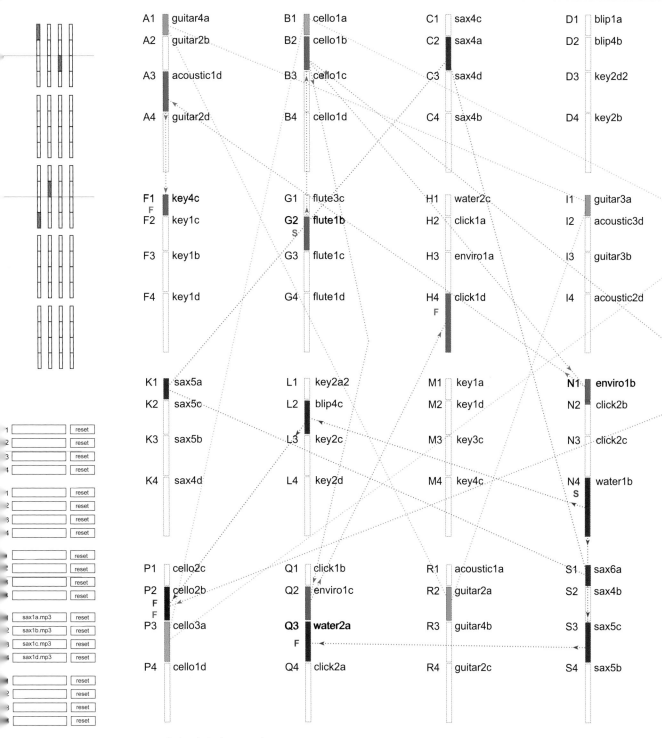

Each pole's four sound samples are networked together, allowing one segment of one pole to trigger another segment of another pole based on pre-choreographed relationships between sound groups.

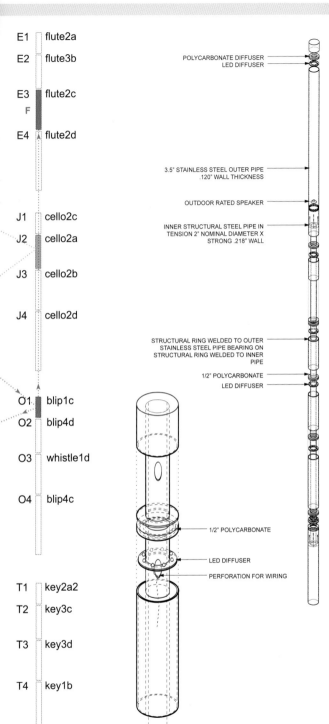

E1 flute2a

E2 flute3b

E3 flute2c
F

E4 flute2d

POLYCARBONATE DIFFUSER
LED DIFFUSER

3.5" STAINLESS STEEL OUTER PIPE
.120" WALL THICKNESS

OUTDOOR RATED SPEAKER

J1 cello2c

INNER STRUCTURAL STEEL PIPE IN
TENSION 2" NOMINAL DIAMETER X
STRONG .218" WALL

J2 cello2a

J3 cello2b

J4 cello2d

STRUCTURAL RING WELDED TO OUTER
STAINLESS STEEL PIPE BEARING ON
STRUCTURAL RING WELDED TO INNER
PIPE

1/2" POLYCARBONATE
LED DIFFUSER

O1 blip1c

O2 blip4d

O3 whistle1d

O4 blip4c

1/2" POLYCARBONATE

LED DIFFUSER

PERFORATION FOR WIRING

T1 key2a2

T2 key3c

T3 key3d

T4 key1b

An inner structure and an
outer touch-sensitive,
stainless steel cas-
ing compose each pole.
The inner structural
pole pulls the segments
together in tension at
the top and bottom.

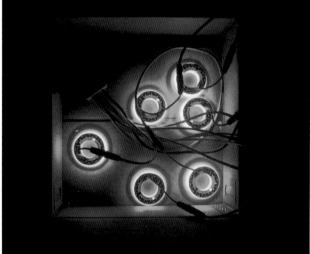

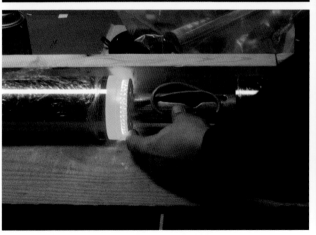

The top of each pole
houses its controller,
MP3 player, and speaker.
Perforations in the
outer pole emit sound.
The hollow cavity
of each pole amplifies
sound internally.

Custom donut-shaped cir-
cuit boards stack flush
with the outer steel seg-
ments. Each board contains
LEDs and is wired to the
pole's controller, which
in turn is wired back to
a central computer within
the adjacent building.

As individual segments of
poles are activated
by human touch, a top cap
of translucent acrylic
flickers brighter to reg-
ister activation that can
be seen from beyond the
immediate site.

PERFORMING PRODUCTION

While the concept of being "wired" is emblematic of progress and connectedness, current conditions of energy production and consumption have reframed public views of electronic technologies. Increased sensitivity to energy use and an emphasis on renewable energy have rekindled an interest in "off-grid" energy sources and applications.

HOVER is a temporary outdoor canopy that harvests energy by day and utilizes that energy for lighting at night. Fabric cells incorporate flexible photovoltaics (PVs), batteries, and light-emitting diodes (LEDs), creating an off-grid lighting system that acts as shelter, shade, and illumination. The geometry for the canopy derives from a pentagonal tiling system of units identical in plan. However, each autonomous cell's conical section orients its PV panel to the sun at its optimal inclination, creating a unique geometry for each cell.

HOVER's light output follows its power intake: after a sunny day, the LEDs will illuminate brightly, while after a cloudy day, the light output will be dim. The project indexes the atmospheric conditions "recorded" throughout the course of the day by transforming harnessed solar power into illumination at night. Drawing renewable energy from the sun, the project highlights ways in which alternative energy can be used to transform urban environments.

HOVER performs both the production and consumption of energy, making its self-contained cycle visible and creating awareness about energy use. It explores public participation in powering off-grid and self-sustaining environments that shelter various forms of public life. As a performative and communicative canopy, HOVER actively engages the zone it demarcates, highlighting the variety of unscripted public activities played out beneath it.

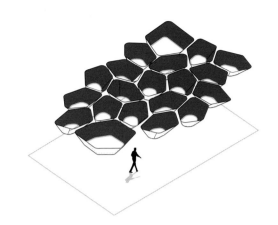

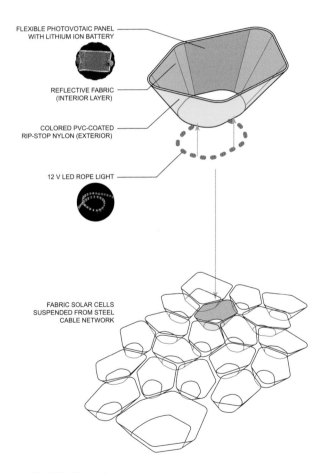

FLEXIBLE PHOTOVOTAIC PANEL
WITH LITHIUM ION BATTERY

REFLECTIVE FABRIC
(INTERIOR LAYER)

COLORED PVC-COATED
RIP-STOP NYLON (EXTERIOR)

12 V LED ROPE LIGHT

FABRIC SOLAR CELLS
SUSPENDED FROM STEEL
CABLE NETWORK

Flexible PV panels
convert sunlight into
energy. The energy is
used to illuminate
the LED rope lights
integrated into each
pentagonal cell.

Viewed at dusk from
below the suspended
canopy, the LED rope
lights create halos
within the lower inner
rings of the cells.

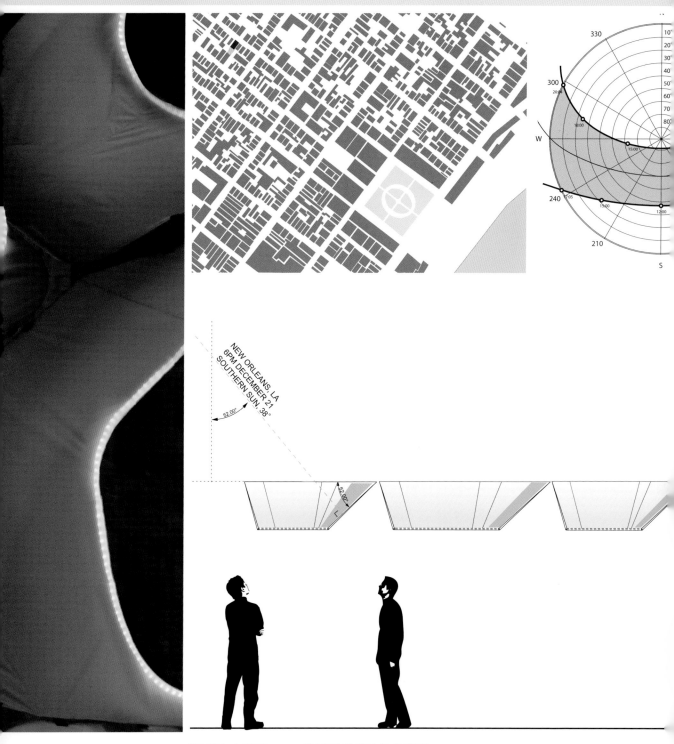

NEW ORLEANS, LA
6PM DECEMBER 21
SOUTHERN SUN, 38°

52.00°

52.00°

The site, a French Quarter residential courtyard, had been turned over to the public as open space for the duration of the DesCours Festival.

The installation is designed specifically for New Orleans in December. Customizing each cell's section based on solar orientation and sun angles maximizes efficiency of the flexible PV panels.

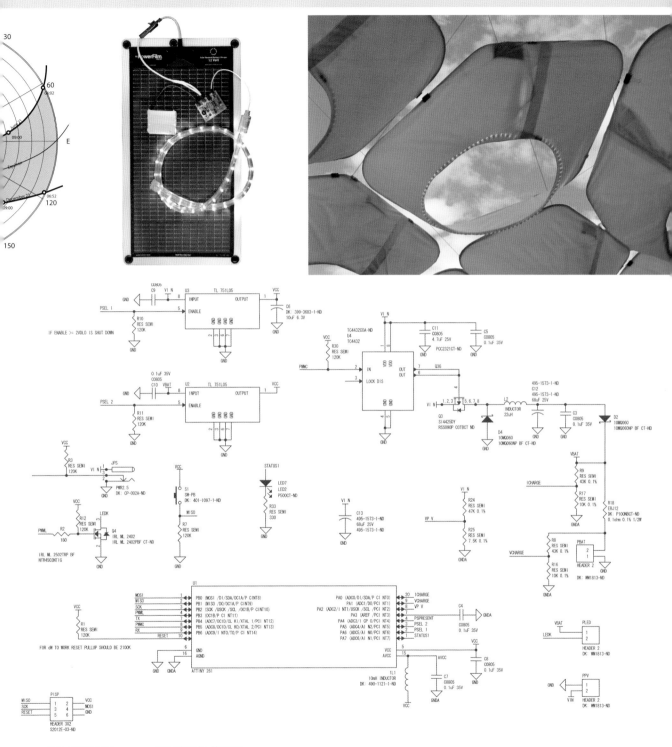

The electronics assembly consists of a flexible PV panel, lithium ion batteries, LED rope light, and custom microcontroller assembly.

The circuit diagram is a representation of the electronic components and their connections.

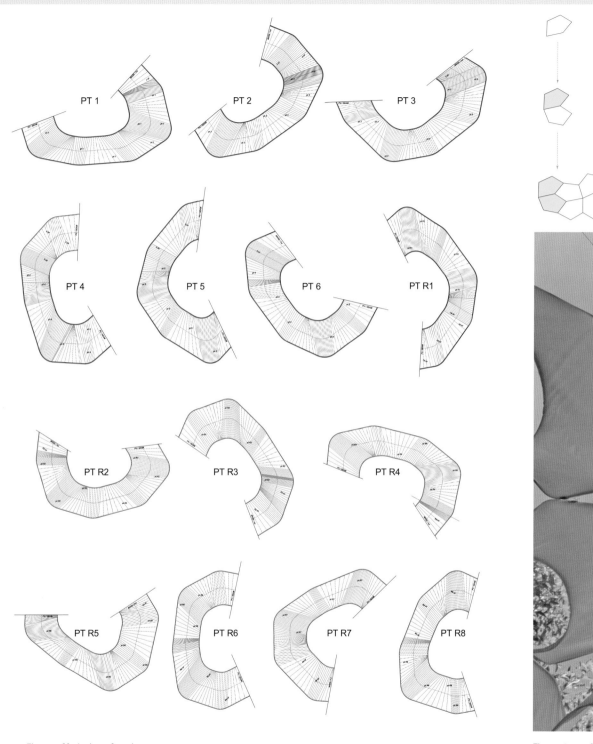

The unrolled view of each cell reveals its individual pattern. While the pentagonal cells are identical in plan, their solar-angle biased sections create a unique three-dimensional geometry for each cell.

The pentagonal tiling system allows the aggregation of cells to accommodate a courtyard of any size.

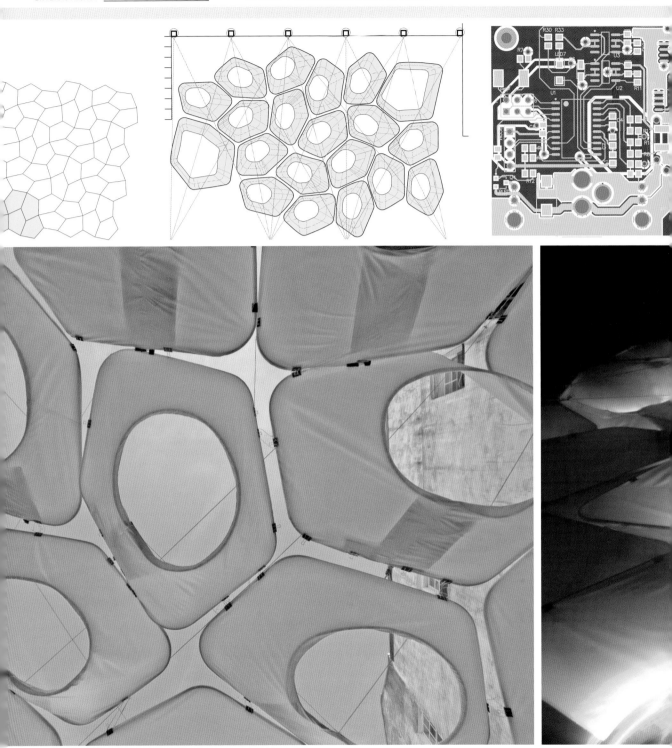

The cells are individually suspended from a cable net system and are structurally and electronically independent of one another.

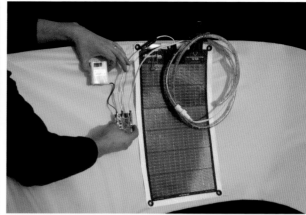

A custom microcontroller controls energy output of the rechargeable batteries at night. The LED rope lights illuminate at different levels of brightness to maximize the use of the rechargeable batteries.

The PV panel acts as a light meter as well as an energy harvester. The controller recognizes when the panel is no longer exposed to sunlight and switches the LED rope lights on.

Cells are made from coated-nylon ripstop fabric. A PV panel is attached to the top surface of each cell and the LED rope light sits in the ring seam below. The weight of the rope light pulls the fabric taut.

Off-grid and self-sustaining, HOVER addresses questions of how we can think of building and rebuilding in sensitive contexts such as New Orleans.

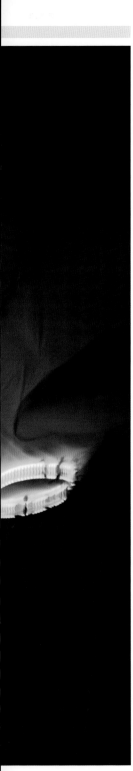

ACTIVATED FIELDS

Sited in Athens at the base of the Acropolis, the responsive environment of WHITE NOISE WHITE LIGHT is tied to a complex historic discourse about the nature of public space. This temporary installation responds in a purposefully playful way, inviting and indexing public participation in an open interactive field.

The project consists of four hundred fiber-optic stalks, emerging out of a raised wooden platform. Custom-designed electronics modules contain passive infrared (PIR) sensors capable of registering the proximity of visitors. When triggered by the sensor, each electronics module delivers a degree of white noise and white light, emitting light through the fiber optics and sound through a small hidden speaker integral to the module. The light and sound increase as visitors approach and decrease as visitors move away. The resulting effect is for each visitor's movements to trigger a sonic and visible wake of their trajectories. Within the field, flickering white lights signal the presence of others, and white noise mutes the sounds of the surrounding city.

Attempting to decode the installation's responsive parameters, visitors experiment with their bodies in the space: running, dodging, stomping, tip-toeing. The static field transforms through their play into an unpredictable aggregation of space, light, and sound. WHITE NOISE WHITE LIGHT explores the idea of public space as one negotiated and defined by its users.

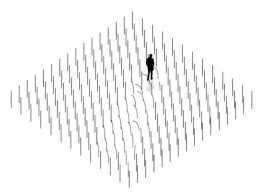

Installed for the 2004 Athens Olympics, WHITE NOISE WHITE LIGHT created an open interactive field of play for an influx of spectators.

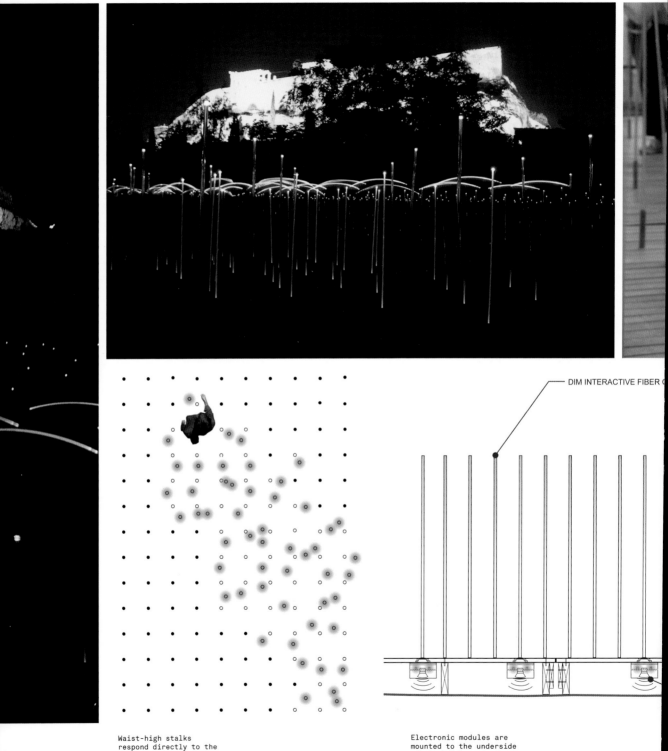

DIM INTERACTIVE FIBER

Waist-high stalks
respond directly to the
presence of each indi-
vidual. The fiber optics
transmit white light as
white noise is emitted
from a module below.

Electronic modules are
mounted to the underside
of the field's raised
deck. Sound is reflected
off the hard surface
of the plaza back up
through the open joints
of the wood deck.

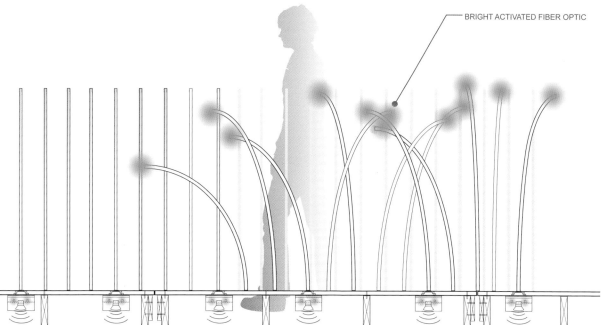

BRIGHT ACTIVATED FIBER OPTIC

SPEAKER EMITTING WHITE NOISE

Fiber-optic stalks are transparent during the day, allowing the sonic component of the installation to become the primary experience.

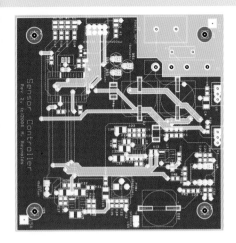

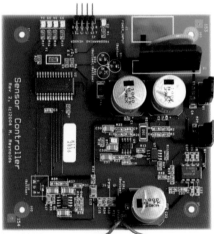

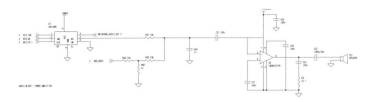

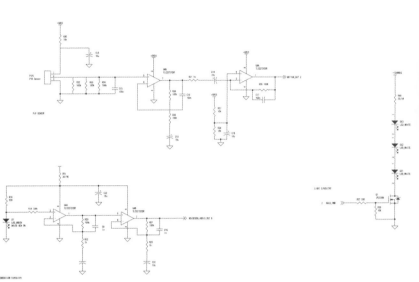

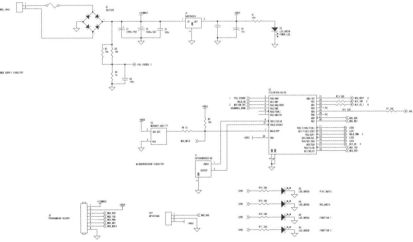

The electronics assembly consists of a custom microcontroller, a PIR sensor, and an outdoor speaker. Each unit is independent of the others and responds specifically to its immediate context.

The custom microcontroller determines illumination levels, sound, and delayed fade behavior. Printed circuit board and controller diagram above is courtesy of Matthew Reynolds.

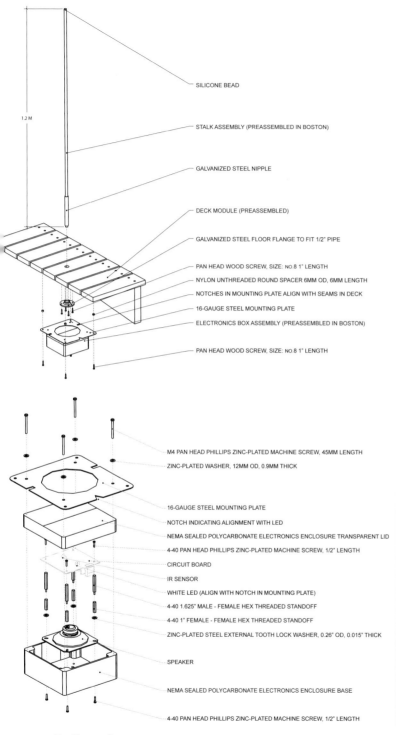

1.2 M

SILICONE BEAD

STALK ASSEMBLY (PREASSEMBLED IN BOSTON)

GALVANIZED STEEL NIPPLE

DECK MODULE (PREASSEMBLED)

GALVANIZED STEEL FLOOR FLANGE TO FIT 1/2" PIPE

PAN HEAD WOOD SCREW, SIZE: NO.8 1" LENGTH
NYLON UNTHREADED ROUND SPACER 6MM OD, 6MM LENGTH
NOTCHES IN MOUNTING PLATE ALIGN WITH SEAMS IN DECK
16-GAUGE STEEL MOUNTING PLATE
ELECTRONICS BOX ASSEMBLY (PREASSEMBLED IN BOSTON)

PAN HEAD WOOD SCREW, SIZE: NO.8 1" LENGTH

M4 PAN HEAD PHILLIPS ZINC-PLATED MACHINE SCREW, 45MM LENGTH
ZINC-PLATED WASHER, 12MM OD, 0.9MM THICK

16-GAUGE STEEL MOUNTING PLATE
NOTCH INDICATING ALIGNMENT WITH LED
NEMA SEALED POLYCARBONATE ELECTRONICS ENCLOSURE TRANSPARENT LID
4-40 PAN HEAD PHILLIPS ZINC-PLATED MACHINE SCREW, 1/2" LENGTH
CIRCUIT BOARD
IR SENSOR
WHITE LED (ALIGN WITH NOTCH IN MOUNTING PLATE)
4-40 1.625" MALE - FEMALE HEX THREADED STANDOFF
4-40 1" FEMALE - FEMALE HEX THREADED STANDOFF
ZINC-PLATED STEEL EXTERNAL TOOTH LOCK WASHER, 0.26" OD, 0.015" THICK

SPEAKER

NEMA SEALED POLYCARBONATE ELECTRONICS ENCLOSURE BASE

4-40 PAN HEAD PHILLIPS ZINC-PLATED MACHINE SCREW, 1/2" LENGTH

The fiber optics are housed in a poly-carbonate tube allowing for flexibility and bending without breaking.

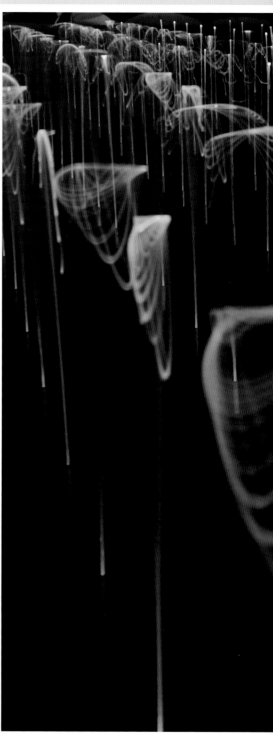

The installation was open to the public twenty-four hours a day for the duration of the Olympics. The use of the field and the number of occupants ranged dramatically from day to night.

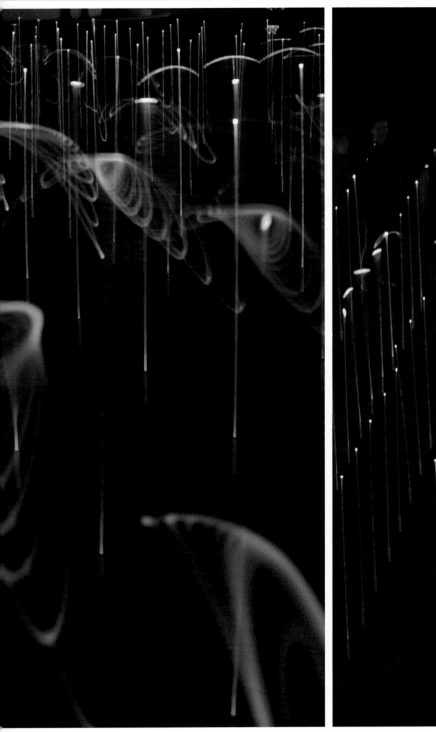

Conceived as an open
field for social interac-
tion, the environment
indexes the movements
of its inhabitants. A
partial reinstallation
at MIT is shown above.

MEDIA

96 97 98 99   00   01   02   03   04

_____ 10,000 m²

_____ 1,000 m²

MEDIA SPILL ⭘

_____ 100 m²

WHITE NOISE WHITE LIGHT

_____ 10 m²

_____ 1 m²

_____ < 1 m²

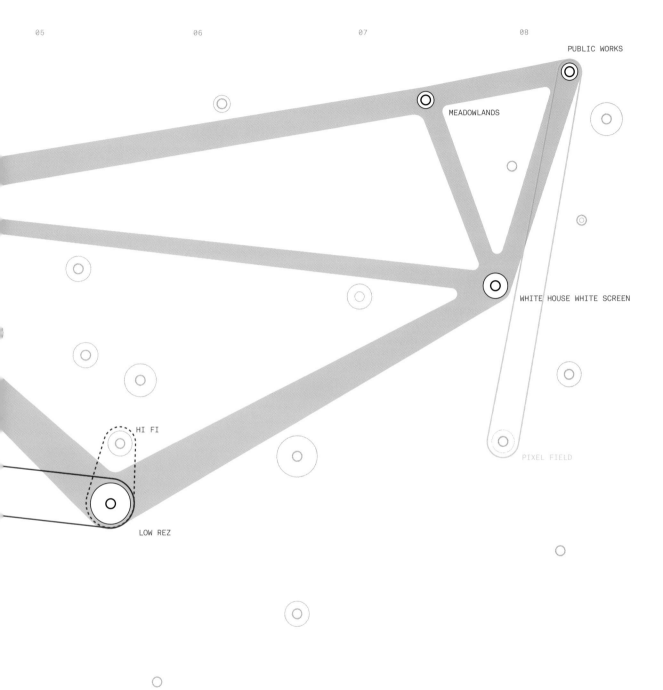

05   06   07   08

PUBLIC WORKS

MEADOWLANDS

WHITE HOUSE WHITE SCREEN

HI FI

PIXEL FIELD

LOW REZ

At its advent, the Gutenberg press displaced architecture as the most enduring broadcast medium. The radical concept of a singular message, mitotically and infinitely divided, gave even the smallest publication a greater reach and permanence than the most monumental of buildings. This shift from monumentality to dexterity and multiplicity foreshadowed the current state of information conveyance, in which the digital—dimensionless and pervasive—dominates as the contemporary media paradigm.

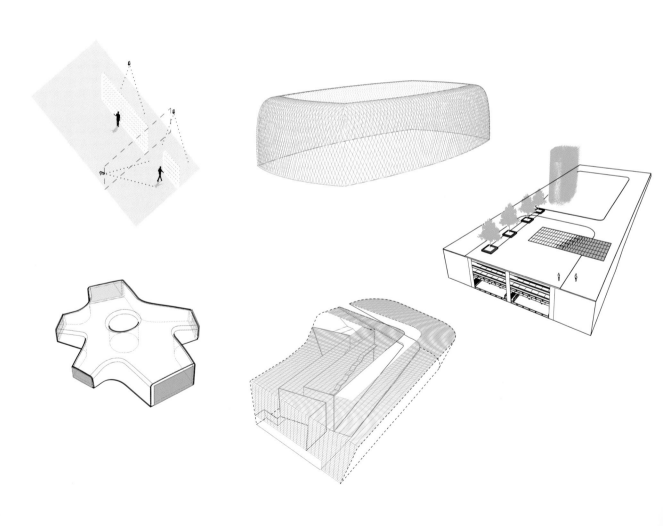

Though information communicated through digital and print media outlasts and outreaches them, the need for physical artifacts, including architecture, has not diminished. Increasingly, architecture incorporates a measure of media and information technology. In fact, architecture itself is a mediating device—controlling, projecting, and branding space. As it is reconfigured by the logics of the port and the terminal, contemporary architecture has the potential to more seamlessly accommodate electronic broadcast technologies.

The current phantasmagoria of media images in contemporary urban centers illustrates cultural critic Walter Benjamin's anticipatory statement in 1936 that architecture is experienced in a state of distraction. The distracting stimuli that Benjamin identified represent only a fragment of the media that proliferate in the public realm today. Architecture—serving as infrastructure, conduit, interface, and icon within the structure of a mass media—participates in the new attention economy.

Newly armed with wireless technologies, the contemporary public occupies a new geography of communication. Online and networked, the public is at once a collection of individuals, a coherent group, and a loosely organic collective. For architecture to engage media in the public sphere, it must also engage the networks of online communities and virtual spaces, drawing connections rather than boundaries between physical and virtual publics.

Further complicating the definition of the public realm is an ambiguity as to how and where this realm stops, who controls it, and how one should behave while within it. The public sphere charted by Vito Acconci in his 1969 Following Piece, in which he followed strangers along New York City streets until they entered a private space, would be complicated by today's shifting boundaries between public and private realms. Increasingly—and particularly after September 11, 2001—commercial and security pressures trespass upon both public and private space.

Our work in architecture and media constructs productive and critical public spaces by acknowledging infringements on the public realm and dealing in the new currency of the image as proliferated through contemporary media. The projects in this chapter explore the increasingly intertwined sets of relationships between producers, consumers, and their interfaces.

Part information display, part signage, and part public art, LOW REZ inserts a series of light-emitting diode (LED) nets into the public realm, broadcasting an overlay of live video feed onto preprogrammed content. The live juxtaposition of "official content" and real-time video, streamed from surveillance cameras, enables the viewer to be an active agent as well as a consumer of public image. WHITE HOUSE WHITE SCREEN acknowledges the omnipresence of media in government, rendering architecture as a backdrop for an edit-ready broadcast. MEDIA SPILL proposes a synthesis between a site strategy based on casting and a media strategy of broadcasting. The building becomes an infrastructure for producing and consuming energy, images, and information.

The projects for the MEADOWLANDS stadium and UNSOLICITED SMALL PROJECTS FOR THE BIG DIG expand the definition of architecture to engage infrastructure, furniture, and signage as an integrated set of mediating elements. Meeting the challenge of temporally transforming a football stadium from a New York Giants to a New York Jets venue, our proposal for the MEADOWLANDS includes a collection of media-based solutions, working with current digital technologies for sports broadcasting, advertising, and branding. UNSOLICITED SMALL PROJECTS FOR THE BIG DIG speculates on the unrealized potentials for Boston's Rose Fitzgerald Kennedy Greenway. Deploying a full range of material and media elements, these projects serve simultaneously as critical commentary and projective speculation, articulating opportunities for a new infrastructural landscape in the middle of Boston.

Recasting architecture as the production of environments to engage the public in larger dialogues, these projects reclaim architecture's place as a primary conduit of information in the public realm. They investigate architecture as a mediating mechanism within the broader cultural phenomena of broadcast and spectacle, and understand architecture as a mass media capable of producing new publics that engage the structures of communication and transmission, transforming participant subjects from passive consumers into active agents.

NET RESOLUTION

Appearing in a range of mediums and scales from an iPhone to a Times Square billboard, information increasingly saturates the public sphere. LOW REZ provides an opportunity for the public to engage issues of surveillance and information overload in the public realm.

LOW REZ consists of a matrix of double-sided light-emitting diode (LED) pixels hung within a glass enclosure. The LED net addresses and engages passersby with its performative and responsive behavior. In its default state, the LED display scrolls the building's address, "1100," across its screen. In its active state, LOW REZ relies on an overlay of public action. Movement along the sidewalk, captured by the building's security cameras, triggers a dynamic response from each of the eight thousand addressable pixels. Walking past LOW REZ, a passerby will notice his or her image broadcast on the LED net—their digital "shadow," superimposed on the streaming "message," allows the body to "erase" the broadcast content.

LOW REZ demonstrates the need for private/public space projects to work on multiple levels. It meets the branding needs of the building owner by engaging the public and simultaneously highlights the mechanisms of surveillance ubiquitous in our society, enabling their public presence to alter the private broadcast content. Superimposing the interactions between the private and public realms, LOW REZ suggests opportunities for agency through performative architectural devices.

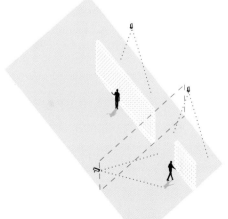

The low resolution and superimposition of live video content of the LED net create a digital shadow and act as a binary electronic mirror.

Content streams from inside to outside, starting with the smallest LED net in the building's elevator lobby, extending into the vestibule and out onto the sidewalk.

The interior LED net separates the entry vestibule from the lobby. As content streams from the interior of the building to the exterior, people move against the "flow" of content.

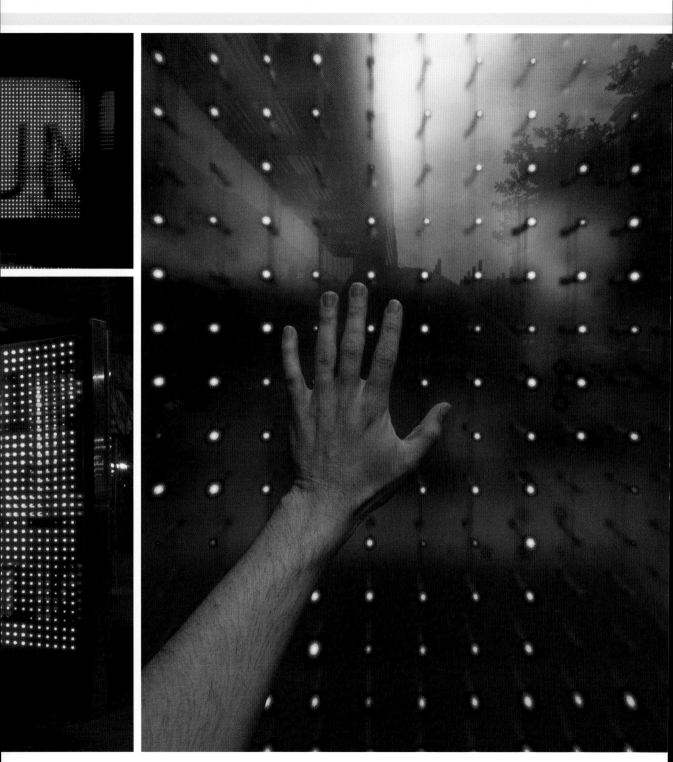

A pixel pitch of 1.5 inches was
determined to achieve both the
recognition of content from a
distance as well as transparency
and abstraction of image through
the net at a close range. The
acid-etched glass diffuses the
LED's light output and slightly
blurs the image beyond.

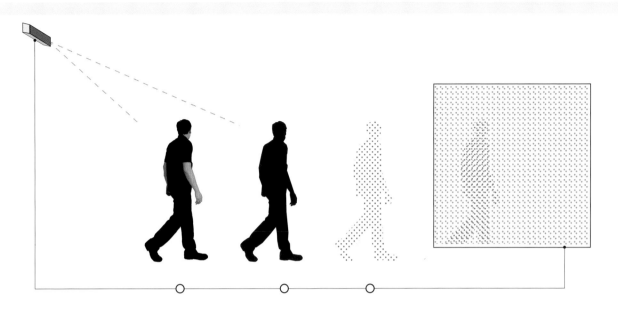

Live feed from the building surveillance cameras capture bodies as they move into and out of the camera's field of vision. The video capture is turned into a high-contrast image and displayed with a slight delay on the low-resolution LED net.

The exterior LED net acts as building signage. The superimposition of a passerby's digital shadow erases the LED net's default content.

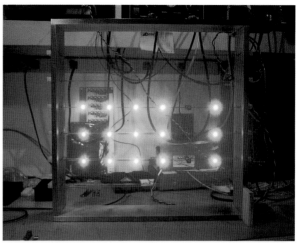

A custom double-sided pixel was designed and fabricated to allow for an individually addressable LED light on each side. The armature for the two LEDs acts as a heat sink.

LED pixels hang from four wires—two providing power and two providing data to each pixel. Wires transmit electrical current and data and act as tensioned support, suspending the LED pixels into a net.

WHITE OUT

If the ubiquitous presence of media renders private lives public, the architecture of the White House is best understood as a public backdrop within which the First Family resides. Less a domestic space than a television set piece, WHITE HOUSE WHITE SCREEN is a carefully crafted tele-optical device.

Continuous, uniformly backlit, smooth-cornered white screens line the house's interior, providing a seamless background on which digital images may be composed in real time. Designed to create an edit-ready domesticity, the exterior geometry anticipates fixed camera locations, choreographed lens angles, and aspect ratios of media outlets. The new White House is not a static icon but the intersection of five cones of vision. A circular interior courtyard provides a sixth focus point anticipating an aerial view. The depthless interiors and media-ready exteriors produce a new kind of executive residence, one perfectly calibrated to the intense stagecraft that is the contemporary presidency.

The "white" in White House exchanges its symbolic value as focus moves from icon to media. No longer representative of purity, hygiene, or acropolitan ideals, "white" is now loaded with contemporary associations. White as an infinite aggregation: white noise, white light, white screen. Whiteness is a by-product of and acknowledgment of overexposure.

Each space within this speculative proposal for the White House acts as a neutral white-screen backdrop that will allow any "context" to be superimposed on the First Family when televised.

Lafayette
Park

Pennsylvania
Avenue Entrance

Visitors'
Entrance

SOUTH

West Wing/
Rose Garden

South Lawn

To enable chroma-key techniques (similar to blue screen or green screen) for mixing two images or frames, all details and corners are removed from the space.

WHITE HOUSE WHITE SCREEN has five facades, each oriented toward a critical point on the White House lawn. Each facade is blank and awaits the context desired by the television broadcaster.

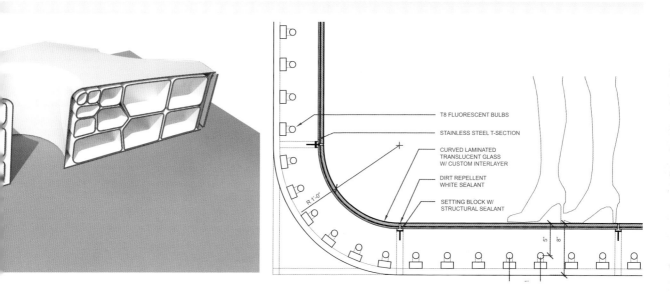

T8 FLUORESCENT BULBS

STAINLESS STEEL T-SECTION

CURVED LAMINATED
TRANSLUCENT GLASS
W/ CUSTOM INTERLAYER

DIRT REPELLENT
WHITE SEALANT

SETTING BLOCK W/
STRUCTURAL SEALANT

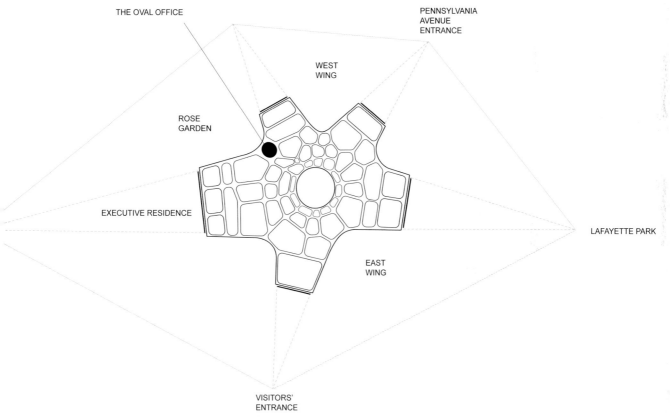

THE OVAL OFFICE

PENNSYLVANIA
AVENUE
ENTRANCE

WEST
WING

ROSE
GARDEN

EXECUTIVE RESIDENCE

LAFAYETTE PARK

EAST
WING

VISITORS'
ENTRANCE

The building plan and
section assume fixed
camera locations, lens
angles, and aspect
ratios of media outlets.
The center is an empty
rotunda.

Various aspect ratios
are used to divide
up the house into
smaller cellular
spaces for the vari-
ous functions of
the White House.

MEDIASCAPE

Although Marshall McLuhan's phrase "the medium is the message" may sound all too familiar now, nearly fifty years after it was coined, the relationships it suggests warrant ongoing investigation. Implicating a "medium" as equal to its content invites a closer look at media as an active rather than passive conduit of information. MEDIA SPILL proposes a synthesis between the static "cast" and the live "broadcast."

MEDIA SPILL casts the residual space of its forested valley site, filling the natural void with its prescribed program, the Nam June Paik Museum. As a literal cast, this project is a congealed, entropic middle ground between program and site, artifice and nature, art and technology. Media, as architecture and ephemera, is deployed and spatialized as both a material and immaterial medium. The roof is the performative surface of the project, its fifth facade. Composed of interchangeable photovoltaic (PV) panels, plasma screens, and glass panels, the operable "curtain-roof" system spans the site, acting as the museum's infrastructural armature.

Two trajectories of movement, separated by speed, cut through MEDIA SPILL. By foot or by car, visitors begin their museum experience by traversing its section. Drive-through and walk-through galleries reflect varying perceptions of movement through space, providing new venues for new forms of media art. MEDIA SPILL conflates the roles of subject and object, producer and consumer, medium and message.

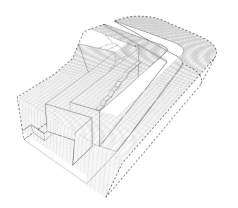

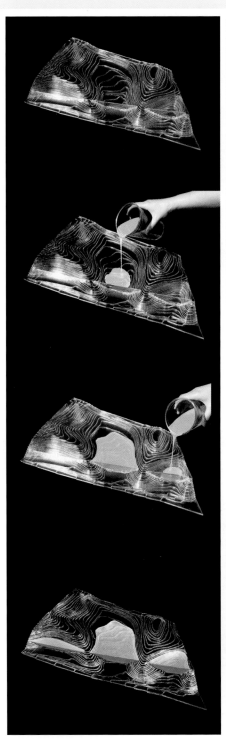

Study models demonstrate the cast nature of the project. Using a liquid that turns into a solid, the model is used to fill the topography of the site with proposed program.

Cars and people must cut
through the museum and its
site in order to park and
enter the building from
above. The form of the
project merges architec-
ture and landscape.

Diagrams reveal program
and circulation volumes,
vehicular movement,
pedestrian movement, and
short circuits through
the museum.

The geometry of the plans and
sections negotiates between
the building program and its
site. Museum circulation
exists for both people and
cars, allowing a drive-through
museum experience before one
enters the museum on foot.

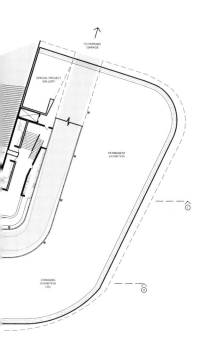

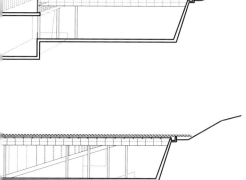

The large, warehouse-like volume of the museum displays media works in an episodic manner through sequential galleries. The circulation frames the galleries, leading viewers from one space to the next.

Galleries are often sandwiched between vehicular and pedestrian circulation, allowing multiple positions for viewing Nam June Paik's media work.

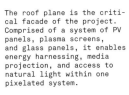

The roof plane is the critical facade of the project.
Comprised of a system of PV
panels, plasma screens,
and glass panels, it enables
energy harnessing, media
projection, and access to
natural light within one
pixelated system.

PV panels line the
museum's roof.
The panels are
angled toward the
sun for optimal
energy harvesting.

SPLIT PERSONALITIES

Architecture and advertising—whose historical relationship has bound one inextricably with the other—find a supersized meeting point in stadiums. These monuments serve as stage sets for the branded broadcast spectacle of professional sports. The new Meadowlands facility in New Jersey boasts a unique double brand, hosting both the New York Jets and the New York Giants. It is the only professional football stadium in the United States to be shared by two teams. Meeting the challenge of temporally transforming the space, experience, and user interface to mediate this split allegiance, MEADOWLANDS looks beyond standard architectural interventions and proposes a collection of media-based solutions.

The designs for MEADOWLANDS range from low to high tech, but all share an understanding that advertising and collective agency can transform a space. The low-tech solutions focus largely on color: blue for the Giants and green for the Jets. Blimp's-eye views could be directed to specific angles to alternately capture a blue or green swath of seating. In a higher-tech proposal, the seats themselves could change color, embedded with colored light-emitting diodes (LEDs). A larger-scale LED solution proposes draping the entire stadium with an LED net, by which a megascale pixelated image could broadcast the correct venue on the stadium's facade. Televised media is engaged by exploiting the line of scrimmage, capitalizing on the current use of the field as a green screen. Co-opting current digital technology for sports broadcasting, advertising and branding are superimposed in a live feed.

Each of these proposals looks outside the traditional domain of architecture and investigates media, lighting, furniture design, and digital interfaces as means of transforming physical space for branded events.

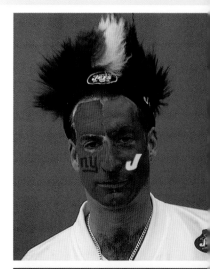

The split identity of the stadium as home to both the Jets and Giants is reflected on a football fan's face, above.

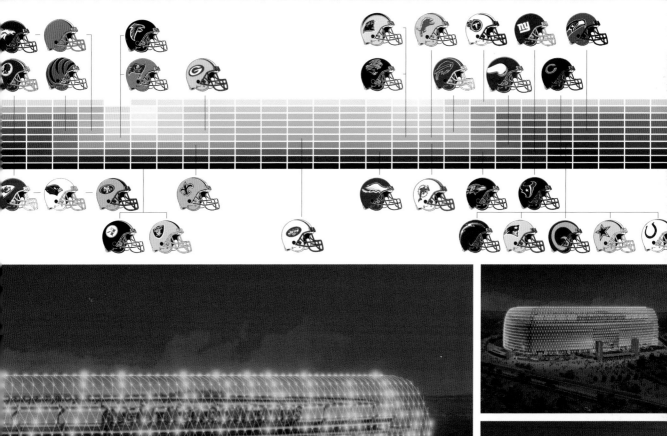

The color chart of NFL teams at top reflects the underusage of green within the spectrum. Asked to study the project for the Jets, we looked at this under-representation as a branding opportunity.

A large LED net draped over the Meadowlands stadium facade allows any content to be displayed at a larger-than-life scale. Jets or Giants identities may be displayed and advertised through a single infrastructure.

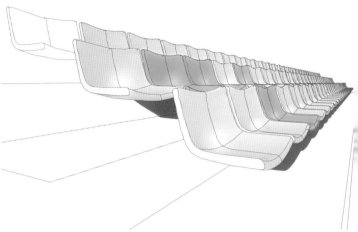

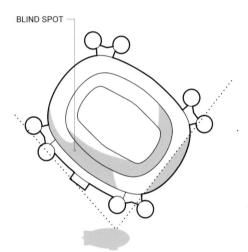

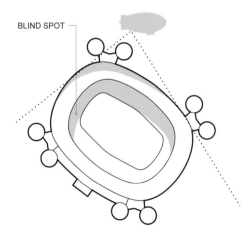

The blimp is used as a television camera platform for aerial views of games. The television rights to broadcast NFL games are among the most lucrative in the business. Static-colored seats can transform the stadium based on the orientation of the blimp.

A slightly more high-tech method of altering the seat color for Jets or Giants games uses LEDs within a translucent plastic seat. The LEDs would be remotely controlled to change color as needed.

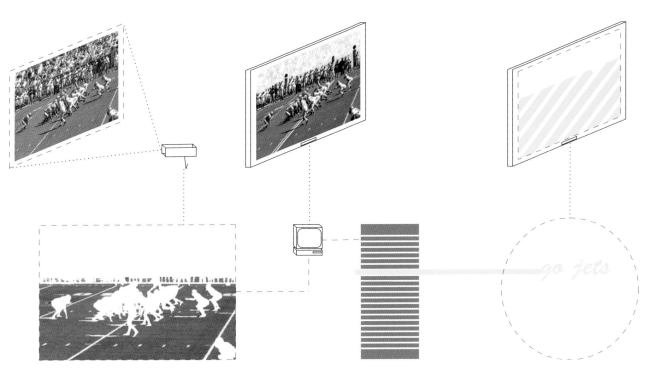

ACTION CAPTURED BY SPECIAL
CAMERAS; TURF ACTS AS GREEN
SCREEN FOR DIGITAL OVERLAYS

TECHNOLOGY USED NOW TO
SUPERIMPOSE GRAPHICS OF PLAY
ONTO TELEVISED IMAGE

A VIRTUAL SITE OF INTERVENTION BY
USING FIELD AS GREEN SCREEN

Green screen is a chroma-key technique
used in sports broadcasting to superimpose a second graphic onto the field.
Using the literal field as a green
screen, the scrimmage line is superimposed electronically. Utilizing this
technology, other forms of identity
and advertising graphics can be added
to the live feed.

INFRA GREEN

Boston's recent addition to its public park system, the Rose Fitzgerald Kennedy Greenway, emerges in the wake of the Big Dig—the massive infrastructural overhaul that relocated the elevated Central Artery to a network of tunnels beneath downtown—occupying a one-and-a-half-mile-long newly exposed surface corridor stretching across Boston's historic peninsula. While Boston's park spaces have historically integrated leisure and functionality (the Fens as tidal sewage filter and Boston Commons as pasture), the current Big Dig/Greenway space presents a strategy of segregation—infrastructure below and park above.

Like a retreating glacier, the completion of the Big Dig reveals a surface dotted with indications of the submerged infrastructure beneath: ventilation structures, traffic ramps, highway signage, and surveillance equipment. Combining information technology, new media, and material innovation with an architectural and landscaping challenge, UNSOLICITED SMALL PROJECTS FOR THE BIG DIG rebuts the existing Greenway's strategy of sweeping its extraordinary infrastructural component under a green carpet.

Several proposed interventions construct an alternative scenario for occupying the Greenway territory by engaging infrastructure. The projects examine a range of temporal scales and draw from a broad group of design disciplines, bringing together architecture, infrastructure, landscape, cultural production, and technology to engage the public.

"Tri-Panel" exploits the simple intelligence of modular image-flipping billboards, a conventional analog advertising technology. Applied to the Greenway's surface at an unprecedented scale—and using asphalt, hardcourt, and turf to compose the three facets of each panel—various surface patterns can accommodate many different programmatic needs.

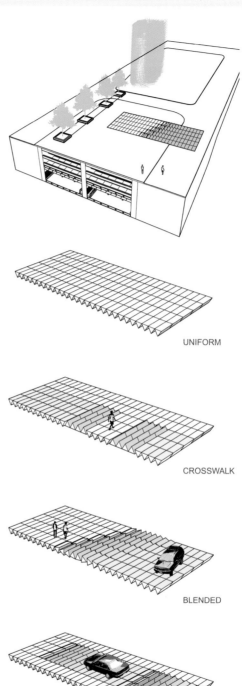

UNIFORM

CROSSWALK

BLENDED

PREDICTIVE

The diagram above shows the various configurations of a tri-panel surface.

The surface of the Greenway
is part road, part lawn,
part sidewalk. Various con-
stituents share this public
space. Tri-Panel imagines a
system that transforms the
Greenway surface based on
program needs.

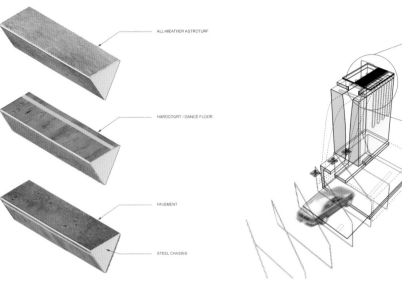

ALL-WEATHER ASTROTURF

HARDCOURT / DANCE FLOOR

PAVEMENT

STEEL CHASSIS

As Tri-Panel's surface transitions between its three states, it creates both barriers between surface zones and views to the tunnel below.

Tri-Panel's three surfaces include soft turf, hardcourt, and pavement. The soft turf is an all-weather artificial turf, hardcourt can be used as a playing surface, and pavement is used for vehicle and bike traffic.

Heat Exchange capitalizes on the steady temperature of the earth below the tunnels with a series of heat-exchanging loops that warm the sidewalks and plaza in the winter outside South Station at Dewey Square.

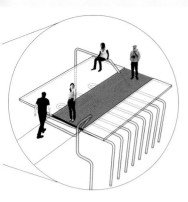

"Heat Exchange" occupies a particularly windswept portion of the Greenway, where Dewey Square sits above the deepest segment of the Central Artery tunnel. A series of heat-exchanging loops uses the steady temperature of the buried tunnels to bring warm air to the surface, creating a geothermal path for the transient occupants of this public space.

"Jogger EZpass" reformats radio-frequency identification (RFID) devices, used by drivers to bypass lines at tollbooths. Countering the disruptive occurrence of intersections along the Greenway, joggers equip themselves with tiny passive-RFID tags worn on the shoe. Jogger EZpass's tags digitally trip sensors in the pavement, which in turn switch traffic rights-of-way in favor of the pedestrian.

"Tree-trap" proposes mechanized planters on tracks embedded in the pavement of intersecting streets. As right-of-way dictates, rows of trees move to create a soft traffic barrier while connecting the parcels together into an unbroken, tree-lined pedestrian crossing.

"Vent Offset" is a parasitic installation that attaches to exhaust-vent structures. Acting both as a security buffer at the tunnel's most vulnerable locations and a filter for the concentrated exhaust from below, the parasite consists of thousands of small-scale quills that use piezoelectricity generated by the airflow-induced mechanical stress on the metal-alloy quills.

These proposals form a critical and creative public space project that is socially, technologically, and physically engaged in addressing the nature and future of the public sphere in our changing global environment.

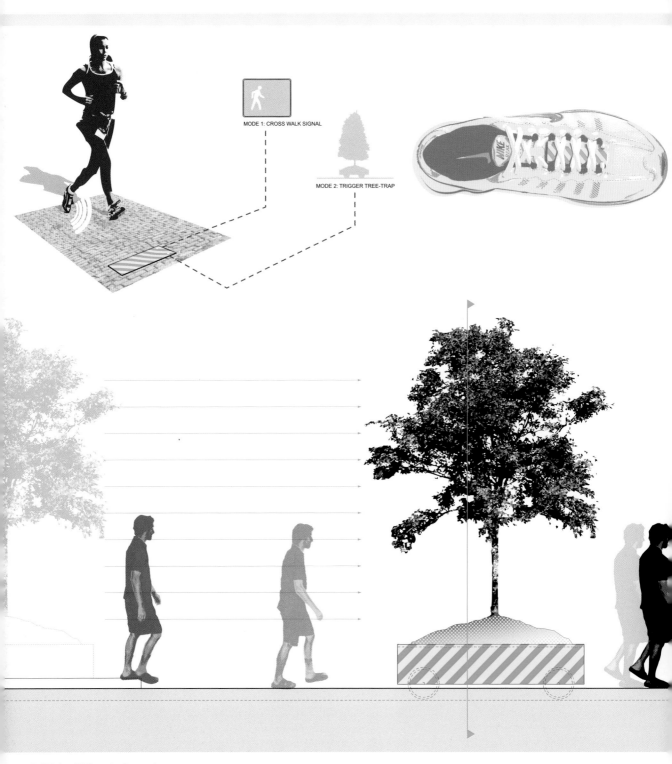

MODE 1: CROSS WALK SIGNAL

MODE 2: TRIGGER TREE-TRAP

Utilizing RFID technology, the Jogger EZpass gives pedestrians and joggers the right-of-way. An RFID tag attached to the runner's shoe automatically trips traffic lights, transforming the Greenway into a continuous recreational experience, uninterrupted by vehicular traffic.

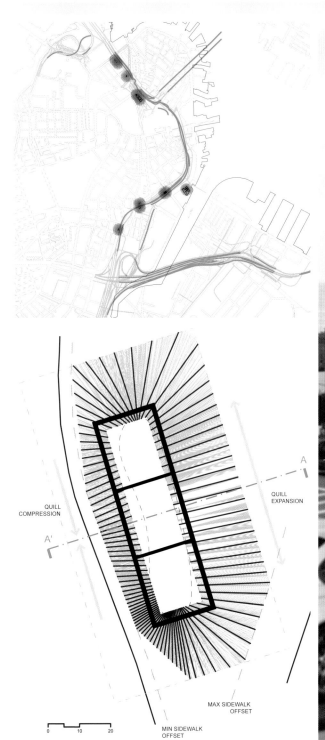

QUILL
COMPRESSION

QUILL
EXPANSION

A

A'

MAX SIDEWALK
OFFSET

MIN SIDEWALK
OFFSET

0   10   20

The diagram at top
maps various inter-
ventions proposed
for the Greenway.

Vent Offset buffers
some of the most sensi-
tive sites along the
Greenway with a protec-
tive and performative
skin of quills.

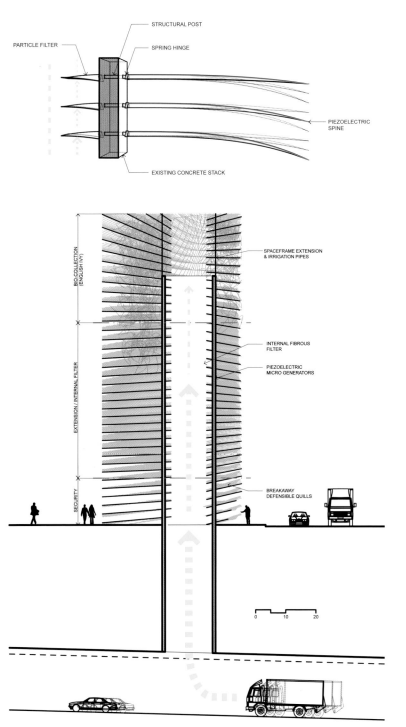

PARTICLE FILTER

STRUCTURAL POST

SPRING HINGE

PIEZOELECTRIC
SPINE

EXISTING CONCRETE STACK

BIO-COLLECTION
(ENGLISH IVY)

EXTENSION / INTERNAL FILTER

SECURITY

SPACEFRAME EXTENSION
& IRRIGATION PIPES

INTERNAL FIBROUS
FILTER

PIEZOELECTRIC
MICRO GENERATORS

BREAKAWAY
DEFENSIBLE QUILLS

0   10   20

Exhaust from the tun-
nel travels up exist-
ing building-sized
infrastructural vents.
Exhaust is filtered
through small quills,
which buffer the vent
and prevent access to
the tunnel through it.

Each quill uses piezoelectricity that is generated by the
mechanical stress of the quill.
Harnessing micromovements generated by airflow in the vent,
the infrastructure becomes a
self-sustaining alternative
energy filter to reduce the tunnel's carbon footprint.

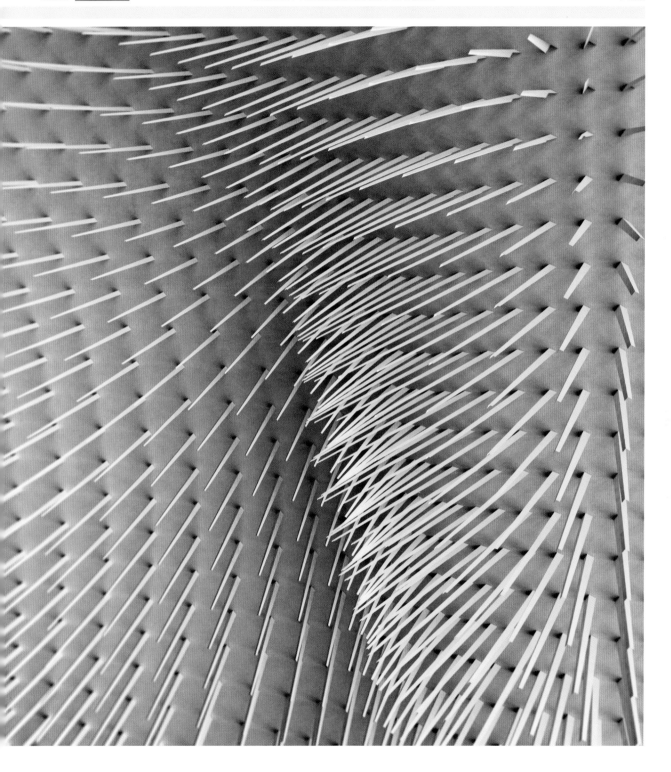

THE SUPERPRODUCERS
Filip Tejchman

Höweler + Yoon Architecture / MY Studio fits the description
of "superproducers": wizards that design from behind
the curtain—tuning, calibrating, and refining—while not
directly engaging in string-pulling puppetry.[1] Rather
than represent the surface residuals and tracery of
performance, their work performs in real time, choreographed and bracketed within certain limits, but sometimes allowed to fall into instability and unexpected
oscillations. They represent a generation that is
not interested in the behavior of one pixel, one control
point, or one spline. Instead, their research-based
projects attempt to predict the effects and habits of
systems and constellations. The superproducer model
refers to the emergence in the music industry of producers whose understanding of software and equipment tran-
scends the act of capturing and recording and instead
extends into the realm of subsuming the original performance and augmenting fidelity. Artists and their
performances become the raw material—their output is
sourced, mixed, dubbed, and processed to create a rich
intertextual and multicultural layering of sound. In
the studio of HYA/MYS, precedents, typologies, and technologies are all subjected to the same calculated dis-
section and transformation. This unrestrained curiosity
avoids the preemptive totalities that limit what can be
researched and how.[2]

There has been a silent shift from thinking about
technology, to thinking <u>like</u> technology. The result is
work that feels organic and even unresolved, but that

is, in its underlying inception, cybernetic and informed by the methods and materials culled from software and CAD/CAM devices. In the case of HYA/MYS, the prototype is the hybrid of these materials and methods, linking their work to the vicissitudes of discourse that flow through academia and practice, but also to the hands-on soldering and programming that they engage in. They have specifically mastered the embrace of contradiction: the overlap and simultaneity of multiple states—both real and virtual—that create what theorist Sanford Kwinter describes as a smectic condition, where form and content are contingent and self-determining.[3]

This conscious interplay between the real and the virtual, between prototypes and concepts, this over-laying of the hard-core of practice with the machinations of material, typifies this generation's definition of a critical practice: one that assigns both content and practice the same level of materiality. It represents a heuristic framework of thought, a way of knowing, that propels a project through the design process but does not emphasize efficiencies of form; rather, it recognizes the innate potential of architecture to bracket the procedure of making against on-the-ground potential. The realization that difference equals value conditions the design process to react to and rationalize the inherent arbitrariness of conditions found in the field—by running the experiment in these conditions, the "wet" prototype eventually supplants the idea.[4]

This is "black-box" architecture, where orchestrated systems working in a virtual framework or infrastructure direct the design process, remaining simultaneously open and constrained. This ambiguity or oscillation between controlled experiment and unanticipated result exemplifies an architecture of objective uncertainty that is dependent on volatility. Through a strategy of aggregated and minute maneuvers, the dimension of time is exploited—looped—occupying a vector of space that fluctuates over time and is laced with possibility. For HYA/MYS, the question is how to manage this disparity between contradictory states in a way that expands on the conception of architectural production.

HYA/MYS have exercised the flexibility of the architectural design process to capitalize on the unexpected limitations of internal constraints such as program and structure and external limits presented by zoning and building codes. This bracketed approach is tuned to seek out the inherent volatility that the design process can manifest. In a sense, it is the willful exploitation of the architects' playbook—to maximize potential without fetishizing the sanctity of form and content. Form is flexible; content is negotiable.

This analytical and self-referencing thought structure—or programming—reaches fruition when it is fed back into the system; while a prototype in the field can verify currents, forces, and every manner of dynamic and static parameter, it is ultimately the transformation of the prototype that is the assumed outcome, the morphing of the model to the reality. However, just as the real and virtual often play surrogate against and with each other, in the case of HYA/MYS, the prototype engages in a reciprocal relationship and eventually provides qualitative information that is then sutured or injected directly into the thought stream of its successor. This genetic genealogy can be seen in the procedural shift that occurs between projects, three of which in particular chart the course of research-specific explorations: Three Degrees of Felt, PS1 Loop, and Entasis.

Three Degrees of Felt (2006), completed and installed in the Solomon R. Guggenheim Museum, has been described as the resolution of the centripetal forces generated by the form and circulation of the building. In terms of procedure, it is the first example of a "scripting" mechanism being employed by HYA/MYS. In this particular case, the "script" is a set of generative moves applied to felt sheets, producing moments of display and site-specific adjustability. As a code, these variations are a subtle and flexible kit of parts that suggests applicability of an idea in any site condition. Determined by the intelligence of this code, the project suffuses and augments the on-the-ground reality, coating the walls and revealing previously unnoticed analytical hieroglyphs: an auxiliary reading or diagrammatic armature of the Guggenheim space.

Of course, it is not a project about scripting; there is no plug-in or line of code that could be installed. Instead, it is a project about thinking about scripting, a dry run or rehearsal in which the structure of the HYA/MYS design process is rethought and acted out like a form of method architecture—self-conscious but reactionary. In this way, the process becomes another mutable parameter in the feedback shake-up. It would hardly be news to suggest that a design studio's process and procedures change and shift with each incoming design argument that is given and each new trait that is necessary to express, essentially motivating the continual redefinition and reexamination inherent in architectural discourse. But what differentiates the HYA/MYS situation is its transparency and deliberate enactment. This bracketing of the unknown and volatile is in a sense the game being played. Moving between scales and fields of operation by hedging the space of the Guggenheim with an adaptable script articulates the results of the experiment as a critical investigation of the latent space.

The "thinking about" scripting analysis that occurred in Three Degrees of Felt is continued in the PS1 Loop proposal (2006). But here, rather than examining the topic of scripting, is a full-blown use of a computer-generated structure, the Voronoi diagram. As a strategy analogous to previously explored idioms of autonomous form in Three Degrees of Felt, PS1 Loop is structurally the same because its two basic ingredients are relatively similar. There is an autonomous, form-generating code and an inflexible, immutable site. Design is the orchestrated dance between the two opposing characters. In a situation where a scaleless and ultimately virtual structure such as the Voronoi is implemented, the critical issue becomes: how does the design process avoid the arbitrary without succumbing to a false rationality?[5]

It is like comparing the Cartesian system invented by René Descartes to the lines and grids of Agnes Martin. Both are meditations on potentials; however, those potentials are characterized as aesthetic versus logic, content versus form, while simultaneously avoiding the arbitrary. HYA/MYS's method is to engage and straddle these differences, bracket them, and allow the experiment to runs its course within a deliberate arena. The rational is manifested in the tuning and minute "dial turning" that contains the behavioral characteristics of the Voronoi within a delineated zone of influence—in this case, the PS1 courtyard site and summer Warm Up program requirements.

The subtle distinction here is that the Voronoi diagram is essentially without a materiality. It does not have the same material intelligence as the felt panels. Although the Loops are eventually materialized and the design augmented by the bend and flex of polypropylene sheets, this is more the resolution of a material question resulting from the initial autonomy of the script than a script informed by these material tendencies. Compared with each other, these two projects demonstrate how the results of each experiment alter the parameters of subsequent design interrogations.

Their installation for the New York Artists Space exhibit Matters of Sensation, Entasis (2008), is similar in its conception to Roxy Paine's SCUMAK (2001), itself an entry in the Greg Lynn-curated show Intricacy (2003) at the Philadelphia ICA.[6] The SCUMAK is a machine that extrudes melted plastic and paint onto a conveyor belt, creating organic and bulbous forms, each unique but also limited to a certain range of fixed variables. The temperature of the material is constant, as is the rate at which it flows from the nozzle; the resulting forms, while varied, are not completely unpredictable. There is not the potential of a radically unique shape. Instead, all the objects possess the same range of instabilities and resemble each other—more or less—within a range of programmed effects. Entasis shares this bracketed oscillation between stable and unstable. Watching it move between states, one witnesses moments when the rigidity of the polypropylene ribbons is compromised as they begin to wiggle at specific points in the rotation.

Here, the results of the polypropylene tests accomplished as part of the PS1 Loop proposal are themselves looped back into the structural proposal, similar to the Three Degrees of Felt process in that material is present first and its limitations programmed into a behavioral logic. The design is based around a series of vertical segments attached to two rotating rings. As these rings rotate, the material bends and produces secondary and ancillary columns within columns. These effects, however categorized, represent a benchmark in the development process because, though the potential genealogy began with codifying the material characteristics of polypropylene, they culminate in a material system that generates forms rather than supplements them. Like the multiple overlapping investigations running parallel in the studio, Entasis is a synthesis of converging explorations and material research with the interactive work HYA/MYS pursues.

While tactics and strategies often emerge as part of a structured process, in the case of HYA/MYS, these tools are simultaneously smooth and striated—a hybridized mash-up of macro- and microcalibrations that channel the bipolar nature of the design development process toward production rather than reflection.[7] Form and structure are emergent when all of the variables are accounted for and allowed to intermingle. Ultimately limited in their range of motion, the process is analogous to a gun going off: there is a combustible explosion that occurs—gunpowder igniting in a chamber—followed by the expulsion of the bullet along an assumed trajectory. HYA/MYS's goal has been to slow down the explosion, to dissect the chain reaction and the careful layout of the smoke, heat, and debris along arcs that—while seemingly familiar—are subtle territories previously unexploited. This is similar to architect Frederick Kiesler's concept of corealism, which can be described as the realization that form is essentially self-generating but contingent on the forces and conditions within which it operates.[8] In a sense, Kiesler's work attempted to extract and make tangible the asymmetrical bracketing created by the convergence of processes with form and the continual rearrangement that this overlap produces.

The simultaneity of these projects is realized by the oscillation between them, choreographing the development of a concept while producing a procedural infrastructure that allows for and stimulates the production of improvisational characteristics. While this is clearly apparent in HYA/MYS's field installation work, such as White Noise White Light (2004) and Hover (2007), it is perhaps best embodied in the hardcore architectural projects.

Building 2345 (2008) has the basic components of an architectural kit of parts—program, structure, and so on—all shuffled, tweaked, and reformed to accept previously untenable modification. In the recent past, cross-programming has articulated and dictated the manner in which architectural mutation would occur: known quantities and known precedents were interposed to produce a programmatic rift. This project, however, is being framed under the FORMATS argument, and the kit of parts idea has been established as safe—not volatile. Instead it is thrown back into the mix, another floating control point against

which to test the proposal. In some terms, it is the most consciously modernist proposal HYA/MYS has made—a relatively generic set of components that are like Le Corbusier's Maison Dom-ino. Both begin as a diagram, a benchmark for an architectural infrastructure that contains programs. Unlike Dom-ino, Building 2345 allows the economics of program to violate its architectural order. Merging the calculative demands of a developer with the spatial programming of an architect, Building 2345 is based on a proposal that is about overlapping mutually exclusive methods. While a developer would necessarily seek to maximize the buildable floor area ratio (FAR)—the maximum amount of square footage allowed on any given site per zoning regulations—HYA/MYS tempers this approach by producing a series of schemes that increase the building envelope while simultaneously creating multiple spatial possibilities, in the form of double-height spaces and mezzanines. In a sense, it is a project without a concept; it is instead the choreography of production with spatial improvisation—a straddle that bounds the generation of space between opposing control points. On one end there is the FAR maximum for the lot, which is bracketed by the FAR bonus available to mixed-use developments; value emerges because of the inherent instability between a set maximum and a floating control point.

A similar twisted logic is employed in the Hayden SRO proposal (2008), where an existing building is supplemented with an exterior circulation/support apparatus. In casing the maximum potential of the existing site, HYA/MYS interweaves similar programs to create a situation in which economic viability is supplemented with incentives backed by the city of Boston. The diagram was developed by finding similarities between outwardly opposed programs. The typical single-room occupancy (SRO) room is less than 400 square feet and is designed to accommodate one person, often with a shared bathroom area. Deceptively similar in size is the programmatic equivalent of a room at the W—a well-known boutique hotel chain—approximately 350 square feet. Because the basic program requirements are so similar, HYA/MYS created a scheme that alternates hotel floors with SRO floors, isolating circulation corridors so the two never connect, but share resources such as mechanical services. As in Building 2345, form is derived rather than invented—the weaving of floor-plans occurs because splitting the circulation would require excess square footage and negate any benefit allotted by the city. More importantly, it is an example of the procedural method used by HYA/MYS—critical in the sense that it represents an interest in balancing formal generation by supplanting it and even privileging pragmatic requirements. Form and content are at all times negotiable, backed against often-perverse programmatic turns of logic. The hard-core projects in particular are invested with a viability bordering on business school legitimacy—historically, close to all-out blasphemy for a critical practice. These are not the Excel spreadsheet design tactics that are currently employed by developers, but there is an underlying script or mechanization that allows for the experiment to run on with a conscious detachment—calibration is done only to maximize results.

For HYA/MYS, the process of practice has become the critical project. It has allowed for the diffusion of professional boundaries, extending the presence of architecture during an economic and social period that has seen the role of the architect diminished and legally compartmentalized. Projects such as Hover and Low Rez Hi Fi (2007) are examples of a design-build methodology, though the term is not an accurate description. Typically, it would refer to an architect that is his own construction manager. However, in reference to HYA/MYS, it represents the normalization of architect as both planner and manufacturer, a conflation of the real and the virtual. It is design-build in a more ephemeral sense, but also an heuristic example reminiscent of craftsmanship, creating a theater of operations that overlaps the processes of practice with the procedure of manufacture. The relationship is often asymmetrical, privileging method or material, instance or event. It is also another example of the contradiction embraced by HYA/MYS that allows for the deployment of multiple methods in concert.

Frozen music is perhaps the most used analogy for architecture, but in an open-source era that has seen the release of music tracks and videos intended for fans to remix, process is no longer held behind-the-scenes or within the privileged realm of the artist.[9] The Rock Star has been overshadowed by the Producer, the mixmaster who controls and directs the performance. It was the Fluxus group in the

mid-1960s that first explored the idea of procedure as performance, though each work was still considered a singular moment—an event unique to itself at each stage of creation. Höweler + Yoon Architecture / MY Studio is extending this generation's definition of a critical practice to one whose methods and materials, the underlying process rather than its results, are the focus of investigation and experimentation.

1. Robert Levine and Bill Werde, "Superproducers," Wired Magazine, October 2003, 126–37. The title for this essay is taken from this article.
2. Sanford Kwinter, "J'Accuse," Praxis: Journal of Writing + Building, New Technologies://New Architectures, Issue 6, 2004, 5.
3. Sanford Kwinter, "Mies and Movement: Military Logistics and Molecular Regimes," in The Presence of Mies, ed. Detlef Mertins (New York: Princeton Architectural Press, 1994), 92.
4. Derived from the term "wetware," originally used by cyberpunk writers such as Rudy Rucker and Neal Stephenson and loosely derived from the cybernetic arguments posited by Norbert Wiener. Wetware is based on the idea that all experience/activity can be broken down into information or software. Wetware, then, is any mechanism for the transfer of software—natural, artificial, or both.
5. Stanford Anderson, "Architectural Design as a Series of Research Programs," in Architecture Theory since 1968, ed. K. Michael Hays (Cambridge, MA: MIT Press, 2000), 490–505.
6. "SCUMAK" derives from Auto SCUlptureMAKer.
7. Gilles Deleuze and Félix Guattari, A Thousand Plateaus: Capitalism and Schizophrenia (Minneapolis: University of Minnesota Press, 1987).
8. Detlef Mertins, "Where Architecture Meets Biology: An Interview with Detlef Mertins," in Interact or Die!, ed. Joke Brouwer and Arjen Mulder, (Rotterdam: V2_Publishing/NAi Publishers, 2007), 110–31.
9. Radiohead and Bjork have both released music videos that allow fans to reimagine and remix the content. In particular, the Radiohead release "House of Cards" comes with a digital file of a three-dimensional scan of the singer's head that can be augmented with a script.

FILIP TEJCHMAN is an architect working in New York City. He received his Bachelor of Architecture at California Polytechnic State University in 2001 and a Master of Science in Advanced Architectural Design degree from Columbia University in 2002. He is a project editor for Praxis and teaches design and drawing at Pratt Institute.

WATCHING IT GROW:
THE INTERDISCIPLINARY PROJECT OF
HÖWELER + YOON ARCHITECTURE / MY STUDIO
Brooke Hodge

When I try to conjure a visual image that could represent
the whole of Höweler + Yoon Architecture / MY Studio's
complex, interdisciplinary practice, I see a kind of
topography with lots of rolling hills, dips, crannies,
hollows, and folds. Traversing this landscape and exploring its spaces, one encounters both hidden places and
open areas full of unexpected surprises—the small conceptual gems, the ingenious interactive installations,
and the larger, ambitious architecture-scale projects.
Yet there is always a connective surface that, by looping
and folding back on itself, converges to knit everything
together into a seamless spectrum of projects that
encompasses the small and the large, the abstract and
the material, the body and the building. In fact, a
fertile landscape is an apt analogy for the work of
HYA/MYS, which includes furniture, dress, exhibition,
book design, architecture, landscape architecture, and
public spaces and installations. Like good gardeners,
Eric Höweler and Meejin Yoon sow seeds of inspiration
to grow their projects. Sometimes a seed will yield
a unique solo offering, but more often the seeds are
fertilized with new ideas and circumstances that spawn
an evolving array of projects and investigations.
    I first became aware of Meejin Yoon's work in the
mid-1990s. She was a student in urban design at Harvard
University's Graduate School of Design, and I was its
director of lectures and exhibitions. Her project for

the introductory urban design studio was selected for inclusion in the annual publication of outstanding student work. The following year she and several other enterprising students launched the journal Paratactics. Hindsight allows me to see the significance of Paratactics for Yoon's subsequent work, both on her own and as a partner in HYA/MYS. The journal's format—bound on both sides (a clever play on the term "double bind," which often refers to a dilemma in communication) and perforated down the middle—actively engaged the reader in the act of reading by forcing him or her to tear the page along the perforation, opening up the book to discover its contents. The notion of transformation through active human engagement continues to be a hallmark of Yoon's work.

Ten years later, I was reacquainted with Yoon and her work when White Noise White Light (her interactive installation for the 2004 Athens Olympics) secured her a spot in the Cooper-Hewitt National Design Museum's 2006 National Design Triennial exhibition. The hand and eye of the architect are present in the spatial sensibility and gridlike organization of the luminous field of fiber-optic stalks that were inserted in a public plaza at the base of the Acropolis. But the beautiful and evocative landscape of light and sound, activated as the field responded to human presence and natural sources, is also the work of an artist. White Noise White Light made me want to look more closely at Yoon's practice and the work she has created in the years since I'd known her as a student.

I discovered an unusual interdisciplinary practice that encompasses conceptual design, public art, furniture, and architecture, to name only a few of Yoon's pursuits. MY Studio, established in 2001, functions like a laboratory where Yoon conducts research, tests ideas, fabricates prototypes, and designs evocative projects in a variety of media not often embraced by architects. Three of MY Studio's early projects are particularly interesting, not only for their creativity and ingenuity but for the way they connect to Yoon's subsequent work and reveal her deep curiosity and eagerness to formulate a project solely as a way to explore an idea or solve a problem. Conceived without the framework of a competition or the guidance of a brief from a client, these projects mark Yoon as a highly motivated independent designer with a keen interest in the way the world works.

Each of these small-scale conceptual projects is an individual object, but rather than being self-sufficient, each demands human engagement to fully reveal the depth of the underlying ideas and the complete nature of the work itself. Absence (2003) is both a book and a sculptural object, designed in response to the World Trade Center Site Memorial Competition. Rather than proposing a traditional design solution, Yoon created an evocative, nonarchitectural memorial that is both portable and personal. At just over two pounds, Absence has a hefty physical presence and a lot of emotional weight. Employing a restrained minimalist strategy, the book is a solid white block of 110 pages—one for each story of the twin towers—and its only "text" is the void of the towers' footprints die-cut into its pages, a ghostly presence of the vanished buildings. As with Paratactics, readers must engage both physically and mentally with the book to discover its contents.

The Defensible Dress (2001) is a one-of-a-kind conceptual project undertaken by Yoon to explore form and performance and public and private space, issues she continues to tackle in subsequent projects. The dress, equipped with sensor-activated, latex-dipped "quills," reacts when it senses another person getting too close to its wearer. The quills thrust out and upward from the body to create what is essentially a protective interactive bustle. Yoon's investigation into the use of new media technologies that—here at the scale of the garment and the body—are activated by human presence to transform a space or environment has continued at a larger, architectural scale in projects including White Noise White Light, Low Rez Hi Fi (a 2006 public project in downtown Washington, DC), and White House White Screen (2008).

Another singular garment design that has had reverberations for several successive projects is the Möbius Dress (2005). Made of white felt, the dress takes the shape of a Möbius strip—a loop with a single, continuous surface, made by flipping one end of a rectangular strip and then connecting it to the opposite end. By cutting while following the contours of the strip two times around, three connected loops are formed. When the cut edges of the dress are zipped together, the garment wraps the body in a stiff A-line shape. When unzipped, the dress unfolds and its intertwining loops cascade to the floor. Yoon's

Möbius Dress can be unzipped and unfolded partially to transform the original shape of the dress into complex curves and loops while still maintaining its continuous surface.

In 2005, Yoon joined forces with Eric Höweler to form Höweler + Yoon Architecture. Höweler, who worked with several large architecture firms including Kohn Pedersen Fox Associates and Diller Scofidio + Renfro, has experience designing large buildings but shares Yoon's interest in conceptual investigations and research. They still maintain MY Studio as a testing ground for research projects and installations, but by this point the boundaries of the two studios are blurred. The question of what is her work and what is his becomes moot, and the work is most often theirs as a team. Now employing several people and moving between scales, Höweler and Yoon have begun to undertake much larger commissions in addition to the competitions and design projects where they can feed their seemingly insatiable appetite for research and ideas. Sometimes they even invent projects because they think something should happen in a certain space at a certain time.

In 2007, Höweler + Yoon Architecture / MY Studio was a finalist in the PS1 Contemporary Art Center's Young Architects competition. Their proposal, PS1 Loop, evolved from Yoon's earlier explorations with the Möbius Dress, but took them to a larger scale and an architectural form. Unlike many previous PS1 projects, HYA/MYS's proposal was not just a canopy or discrete architectural object to be placed in the courtyard in front of the art center, once a public school. Rather, they created an immersive social environment that could serve as a scaffold for the various activities that take place in the courtyard over the course of a summer. Part landscape and part infrastructure, PS1 Loop is a pliable polypropylene latticework that allows for both complete porosity and total coverage—once again, an investigation into the notion of public space. The lower surfaces are curved, contoured, and reinforced for lounging while the upper canopy provides generous shade and dramatic shadows. Performative activity clusters—waterfalls, a foam chamber, and bubble jets—activated by motion sensors enable the environment to respond to its occupants. The geometry of PS1 Loop is generated from an analysis of cellular aggregates, suggesting an uninterrupted organizational system that outlines connections between spaces but never completely encloses or exposes them. Like many architects of their generation, Höweler and Yoon are intrigued by the intersection between computation and craft. While the geometry of PS1 Loop is controlled through computational tools, its final form is dependent on manual assembly.

Though HYA/MYS did not win the competition, they weren't content to let Loop languish and, returning to the scale of the single body, soon turned its generative idea into a design for a chair. As yet only prototypes, the Loop Chairs are contoured by the body and conceived as single closed ribbons, again harking back to the idea of the Möbius strip. Made of flexible polypropylene sheets that are heat-formed over wooden molds, the chairs are shaped into both sitting and reclining surfaces.

These projects reveal the continuous looping process that underlies Höweler and Yoon's practice. No project lies fallow even if it remains a prototype, every seed of an idea suggests another, and most have echoes in subsequent projects. With the partners moving into the design of larger-scaled buildings—houses, a hotel, and a mixed-use complex, to name a few—one can imagine the complex interdisciplinary projects that lie ahead as they plant and reap new fields of ideas. I like to think—with their interest in furniture design, textiles, and complex patterns—that they might follow some of the important figures of the early twentieth century, such as Charles and Ray Eames, who designed every aspect of an environment: from the building, to its furniture, to the clothes worn by its occupants.

BROOKE HODGE is Curator of Architecture and Design at the Museum of Contemporary Art in Los Angeles. From 1991–2000 she was Director of Exhibitions and Publications at the Harvard University Graduate School of Design. She has organized exhibitions of the works of architects Frank Gehry, Gio Ponti, Zaha Hadid, Kazuyo Sejima, Enric Miralles, theater designer and artist Robert Wilson, car designer J Mays, and fashion designer Rei Kawakubo, among others. Her most recent MOCA exhibition project, Skin + Bones: Parallel Practices in Fashion and Architecture, was presented in Los Angeles, Tokyo, and London, and she is currently working on exhibitions of the works of Morphosis and Ball-Nogues Studio, which will open at MOCA in 2009. Hodge is a contributor to Wallpaper and also writes "Seeing Things," a biweekly design column for "The Moment," the New York Times Magazine's blog.

PROJECT CREDITS

PARATACTICS
Cambridge, MA, 1996
Scope: student journal at Harvard University
Graduate School of Design
Project Team: J. Meejin Yoon, Srdjan Janovic
Weiss, Yenna Chan

HYBRID CARTOGRAPHIES
Seoul, Korea, 1997
Scope: artist book
Author: J. Meejin Yoon
Support: Fulbright Scholarship

DEFENSIBLE DRESS
Cambridge, MA, 2001–2006
Scope: concept clothing
Project Team: J. Meejin Yoon, Daniel Cho,
Daniel Smithwick, Saran Oki
Electronics Engineer: Matt Reynolds

MEDIA SPILL
Seoul, Korea, 2003
Scope: Nam Jun Paik Museum competition
Collaborator: Franco Vairani
Project Team: J. Meejin Yoon, Tim Morshead,
Rori Dajao

PLEATED WALL
New York, NY, 2003
Scope: display wall
Project Team: J. Meejin Yoon, Kyle Steinfeld,
Tim Morshead, Amy Yang, Cathy Kim
Electronics Engineer: Matthew Reynolds

ABSENCE
New York, NY, 2003
Scope: artist book
Publisher: Printed Matter and the Whitney
Museum of American Art
Author: J. Meejin Yoon
Support: New York City Department of Cultural
Affairs, Andy Warhol Foundation of the Visual
Arts, Elizabeth Firestone, Graham Foundation,
Heyday Foundation

COUNTER BALANCE
New York, NY, 2003
Scope: exhibition design
Client: Center for Architecture, AIA New York
Chapter
Project Team: J. Meejin Yoon, Eddie Chiu-Fai Can,
Marlene Kuhn, Milena Tsvetkova, Jon Braddock

THREE DEGREES OF FELT
New York, NY, 2004
Scope: exhibition design for Aztec Empire
show at the Solomon R. Guggenheim Museum
Collaborator: Enrique Norten / TEN Arquitectos
MY Studio Team: J. Meejin Yoon, Tim Morshead,
Stylianos Dristas, Alex Miller, Shuji Suzumori,
Kyle Steinfeld, Carl Solander
Computation: Styliano Dristas

WHITE NOISE WHITE LIGHT
Athens, Greece, 2004
Scope: public art installation
Client: Athens 2004 Olympic Committee
Project Team: J. Meejin Yoon, Marlene Kuhn,
Kyle Steinfeld, Lisa C. Smith, Naomi Munro,
Eric Höweler
Electronics Engineer: Matthew Reynolds

MÖBIUS DRESS
Cambridge, MA, 2004–2005
Scope: concept clothing
Project Team: J. Meejin Yoon, Lisa C. Smith

BUILDING 2345
Washington, DC, 2005–2008
Scope: mixed-use building (8,250 s.f.)
Client: 2345 MLK, LLC
Project Team: J. Meejin Yoon, Eric Höweler,
Carl Solander, Liz Burrow, Daniel Smithwick
Structural Engineer: MGV
Mechanical Engineer: MEP Tech

TRIO
Palisades Park, NJ, 2005–2007
Scope: public-space interiors (30,000 s.f.)
Client: Tarragon Development Corporation
Project Team: J. Meejin Yoon, Eric Höweler,
Carl Solander, Lisa C. Smith, Meredith Miller,
Gerri Davis

TRIPLE HOUSE
McLean, VA, 2005
Scope: residence (4,500 s.f.)
Client: withheld
Project Team: J. Meejin Yoon, Eric Höweler,
Carl Solander, Meredith Miller, Yusun Kwon

LOW REZ HI FI
Washington, DC, 2005–2007
Scope: interactive public space
Client/Collaborator: Abbott Stillman,
Stillman Group
Project Team: J. Meejin Yoon, Eric Höweler,
Carl Solander, Lisa C. Smith, Meredith Miller,
Yusun Kwon, Saran Oki
Electronics Engineer: Will Pickering, Parallel
Development

WOLK GALLERY
Cambridge, MA, 2005
Scope: exhibition
Venue: Massachusetts Institute of Technology
Project Team: J. Meejin Yoon, Lisa C. Smith,
Carl Solander, Sawako Kaijima, Shuji Suzumori

NET X-INGS
Chicago, IL, 2006
Scope: competition for pedestrian bridge,
third prize
Sponsor: Chicago Architectural Foundation
Project Team: J. Meejin Yoon, Eric Höweler,
Carl Solander, Meredith Miller
Collaborator: Paul Kassabian PE, Simpson
Gumpertz & Heger

PS1 LOOP
New York, NY, 2006
Scope: Young Architects Program, finalist
Client: MoMA / PS1
Project Team: J. Meejin Yoon, Eric Höweler,
Jimmy Shen, Saeed Arida, John Snavely, Orlin
Zhekov, Daniel Yi-Hsiang Chao, Carl Solander,
James Smith, Lisa C. Smith
Structural Engineer: Markus Schulte PE, ARUP

BRIDGE HOUSE
McLean, VA, 2006–2008
Scope: single-family residence (6,500 s.f.)
Client: Mr. and Mrs. Chung
Project Team: J. Meejin Yoon, Eric Höweler,
Meredith Miller, Carl Solander, Joe Michael
Structural Engineer: MGV
Mechanical Engineer: MEP Tech

LOOSE FILL
Providence, RI, 2006
Scope: exhibition, Rhode Island School of Design
Project Team: J. Meejin Yoon, Eric Höweler,
Meredith Miller, Carl Solander, Daniel Smithwick

ONE DPI
Boston, MA, 2006
Scope: exhibition, Northeastern University
Project Team: J. Meejin Yoon, Eric Höweler,
Carl Solander, Lisa C. Smith

LOOP CHAIRS
Boston, MA, 2006
Scope: furniture prototype
Project Team: J. Meejin Yoon, Eric Höweler,
Carl Solander, Jimmy Shen, Daniel Smithwick,
James Smith, Andrew Todd Marcus

TRAVEL REPORTS
Cambridge, MA, 2006
Scope: book design
Client: The Architectural League of New York
Project Team: J. Meejin Yoon, Lisa C. Smith

DA ZHONG LI
Shanghai, China, 2007–2008
Scope: mixed-use complex, design consultant
(3,000,000 s.f.)
Associate Architect: Wong & Ouyang HK (LTD)
Project Team: Eric Höweler, J. Meejin Yoon,
Matt Chua, Meredith Miller, Casey Renner

MEADOWLANDS
Meadowlands, NJ, 2007–2008
Scope: temporal branding
Client: Three Square Consulting
Project Team: J. Meejin Yoon, Eric Höweler,
Meredith Miller, Daniel Cho, Ryan Murphy,
Ryan Pinkham, John Snavely

BOSTON CITY HALL 2.0 Wrap / Sleeve
Boston, MA, 2007
Scope: project for print, Architecture Boston
Magazine
Project Team: Eric Höweler, J. Meejin Yoon,
Carl Solander, Meredith Miller, Teddy Huyck

WHITE HOUSE WHITE SCREEN
Washington, DC, 2008
Scope: competition entry, White House Redux
Project Team: J. Meejin Yoon, Eric Höweler,
Meredith Miller, Casey Renner, Saran Oki

NEW BEDFORD BOATHOUSE
New Bedford, MA, 2007–2008
Scope: community boathouse (10,000 s.f.)
Client: City of New Bedford
Collaborators: MIT Design Build Studio, Fall 2007
Project Team: J. Meejin Yoon, Eric Höweler,
James Graham, Ryan Murphy, Andrew Wit,
Colin Kerr, Thaddeus Jusczyk
Structural Engineers: Matthew Johnson and
Paul Kassabian, Simpson Gumpertz & Heger

OUTSIDE IN LOFT
Boston, MA, 2007
Scope: loft renovation (2,200 s.f.)
Client: Sam and Leslie Davol
Project Team: J. Meejin Yoon, Eric Höweler, Carl
Solander, Elizabeth Christoforetti, Teddy Huyck
Contractor: Benjamin Construction
Structural Engineer: Sarkis Zerounian
Mechanical Engineer: Sinote Ibrahim

HOVER
New Orleans, LA, 2007
Scope: temporary public-space installation
(900 s.f.)
Client: AIA New Orleans Chapter
Project Team: J. Meejin Yoon, Eric Höweler,
Meredith Miller, Daniel Cho, Gabriel Cira,
Lizzie Krasner
Electronics Engineer: Will Pickering,
Parallel Development
Structural Engineer: Paul Kassabian,
Simpson Gumpertz & Heger

LIGHT LOOM
Boston, MA, 2007–2008
Scope: site-specific art installation (600 s.f.)
Client: Millennium Partners, Boston
Project Team: J. Meejin Yoon, Eric Höweler,
Meredith Miller, Daniel Cho, Ryan Pinkham

UNSOLICITED SMALL PROJECTS FOR THE BIG DIG
Boston, MA, 2008
Scope: project for print publication
Project Team: J. Meejin Yoon, Eric Höweler,
Meredith Miller, Buck Sleeper, Ryan Murphy,
Saran Oki, Joe Michael, Casey Renner, Matt Chua,
Jennifer Chuong
Support: Graham Foundation Production and
Presentation Research Grant, MIT HAAS Grant

SKY COURTS COMPLEX
Chengdu, China, 2008
Scope: corporate headquarters club building
(20,000 s.f.)
Client: withheld
Project Team: J. Meejin Yoon, Eric Höweler,
Meredith Miller, Matt Chua, Casey Renner,
Jennifer Chuong, Nerijus Petrokas, Saran Oki

HAYDEN SRO
Boston, MA, 2008
Scope: housing feasibility study (20,000 s.f.)
Client: Asian Community Development
Corporation
Project Team: J. Meejin Yoon, Eric Höweler,
Ryan Murphy, Meredith Miller, Ryan Pinkham
Support: Bemis Award

HOTEL ΔT
Tiverton, RI, 2008
Scope: boutique hotel and spa (11,000 s.f.)
Client: Nonquit Realty
Project Team: J. Meejin Yoon, Eric Höweler,
Casey Renner, Matt Chua
Structural Engineer: St. Jean Engineering
Mechanical Engineer: Creative Environment Corp.

CLIFF STREET HOUSE
Ithaca, NY, 2008
Scope: single-family house
Client: Kim Dupcak
Project Team: J. Meejin Yoon, Eric Höweler,
Ryan Murphy, Joe Michael

TOPO LOUNGE
Boston, MA, 2008
Scope: public-space interiors
Client: Millennium Partners, Boston
Project Team: J. Meejin Yoon, Eric Höweler,
Meredith Miller, Casey Renner, Matt Chua

PIXEL FIELD
Boston, MA, 2008
Scope: public-space installation
Collaborators: Ground, LinOldham Office,
Merge Architects, MOS, over,under, SSD,
Studio Luz Architects, Utile, UNI
HYA Team: J. Meejin Yoon, Eric Höweler, Meredith
Miller, Casey Renner, Ryan Pinkham, Minsoo Lee,
Kate Cho

ENTASIS
New York, NY, 2008
Scope: site-specific kinetic installation, Matters
of Sensation exhibition, Artists Space Gallery
Curators: Marcelo Spina, Georgina Huljich
Project Team: J. Meejin Yoon, Eric Höweler,
Meredith Miller, Casey Renner, Nerijus Petrokas,
Minsoo Lee, Ryan Pinkham
Electronics Engineer: Will Pickering, Parallel
Development

SELECTED BIBLIOGRAPHY

By HYA/MYS

Höweler, Eric, and J. Meejin Yoon. 1,001 Skyscrapers. New York: Princeton Architectural Press, 2000.

Höweler, Eric. Skyscraper: Vertical Now. New York: Universe, 2004.

Yoon, J. Meejin. Absence. New York: Printed Matter, Inc. & the Whitney Museum of American Art, 2004.

Yoon, J. Meejin. "emBodied Tectonics." In Material Process: Young Architects 4, by Architectural League of New York, 124–49. New York: Princeton Architectural Press, 2003.

Yoon, J. Meejin. Hybrid Cartographies: Seoul's Consuming Spaces. Seoul: J. Yoon, 1998.

Yoon, J. Meejin. "(K)not a Loop." In AD Elegance, 86–7. West Sussex, England: Wiley-Academy, 2006.

Yoon, J. Meejin. "Programming Scenarios: R&Sie." Praxis: Writing + Building 8 (2006): 73–81.

Yoon, J. Meejin. "Public Works, Projects at Play." Journal of Architectural Education (Spring 2008): 59–68.

On HYA/MYS

1000x Architecture of the Americas, 165–66. Berlin: Verlagshaus Braun, 2008.

"Annual Design Review." I.D. Magazine (July 2004).

"R + D Award." Architect Magazine (August 2008).

Bernstein, Fred A. "Quitting their Day Jobs and Scaling Up." New York Times, November 22, 2007.

Brownell, Blaine. Transmaterial 2: A Catalog of Materials That Redefine Our Physical Environment. New York: Princeton Architectural Press, 2008.

Cullerton, Erin, ed. Young Architects Americas. Cologne, Germany: DAAB, 2007.

Donoff, Elizabeth. "Urban Instrument." Architecture Lighting (June 2007).

Kennicott, Philip. "Bathed in the Right Light." Washington Post, August 26, 2007.

Payne, Andrew. "Surfacing the New Sensorium." Praxis: Writing + Building 9 (October 2007).

Sokol, David. "When Mardi Gras Came Early." Interior Design Magazine (February 2008).

Stephens, Suzanne. "Höweler + Yoon blurs edges between art and architecture with digital aplomb." Architectural Record (December 2007).

Temin, Christine. "A Shining Example of Adventurous Art." Boston Globe, May 4, 2005, sec. C1.

Weisstuch, Liza. "Thinking Outside and Inside the Box." Boston Globe, May 15, 2008.

SELECTED EXHIBITONS

Matters of Sensation
Artist Space, New York, NY, 2008

Skin + Bones: Parallel Practices in Fashion and Architecture
Somerset House, London, UK, 2008
The National Art Center, Tokyo, Japan, 2007
The Museum of Contemporary Art, Los Angeles, CA, 2006

Design Life Now: National Design Triennial
Contemporary Arts Museum, Houston, TX, 2008
Institute of Contemporary Art, Boston, MA, 2007
Cooper-Hewitt Museum, New York, NY, 2006

Unravel: SIGGRAPH 2006
Thirty-third International Conference and Exhibition on Computer Graphics and Interactive Techniques, Boston, MA, 2006

The Big Nothing
Institute of Contemporary Art, Philadelphia, PA, 2004

MCA Artists' Book collection
Museum of Contemporary Art, Chicago, IL, 2004

Material Process: Young Architects
Architecture League of New York, NY, 2002

A Century of Innovative Book Design
American Institute of Graphic Art, New York, NY, 1999

BIOGRAPHIES

Höweler + Yoon Architecture / MY Studio is an expanded architectural practice, grounded in the discipline of architecture but not limited by its boundaries. Engaging practice as a series of applied research agendas, they seek to test ideas at multiple scales and across different disciplinary territories: architecture, art, landscape, lighting, and interactive design. They are interested in the material realities and material effects of their work, testing ecologies of interactions between their constructs and the larger public. As architects, situated against the backdrop of accelerating ecological, informational, technological, and cultural connectedness, they recognize the need for architects to become active participants in the production of this evolving, interconnected environment.

HYA/MYS were awarded the Architecture League's Emerging Voices award and named as an Architectural Record Design Vanguard in 2007. Their recent interactive architecture/landscape projects were featured in the 2006 National Design Triennial at the Cooper Hewitt National Design Museum in New York. Their work has also been included in exhibitions at the Los Angeles Museum of Contemporary Art, the Museum of Modern Art in New York, and the Museum of Contemporary Art in Chicago. The work of HYA/MYS has been nationally and internationally recognized, published, and reviewed.

J. MEEJIN YOON (b. Seoul, Korea) is an architect, designer, and educator. She received a Bachelor of Architecture from Cornell University with the AIA Henry Adams Medal, and a Master of Architecture in Urban Design with Distinction from Harvard University. She is an associate professor at Massachusetts Institute of Technology and founder of MY Studio in 2001 and Höweler + Yoon Architecture in 2005. She is the recipient of the 2008 United States Artist fellowship, the 2008 Athena RISD/Target Emerging Designer Award, the 2005 Rome Prize in Design, the 2002 Young Architects Award from the Architectural League New York, and a Fulbright Fellowship for Independent Research in 1997. She is the author/designer of Absence, a World Trade Center Memorial artist book published by Printed Matter and the Whitney Museum of American Art in 2003.

ERIC HÖWELER (b. Cali, Colombia) is a registered architect with thirteen years of experience in practice. He received a Bachelor of Architecture and a Master of Architecture from Cornell University. He is currently a design critic at the Harvard University Graduate School of Design. Prior to forming Höweler + Yoon Architecture, Eric was a senior designer at Diller + Scofidio, and an associate principal at Kohn Pedersen Fox Associates. He is the author of Skyscraper: Vertical Now, published by Rizzoli/Universe Publishers in 2004.

ACKNOWLEDGMENTS

We are grateful to the numerous extraordinary, talented, and intelligent people that have worked with us over the years. The work included in this book is the product of the collaborative ecology of the studio—where ideas and concepts are authored and developed in a context of discussion and debate. Members of the studio have included: Carl Solander, Lisa C. Smith, Meredith Miller, Matt Chua, Casey Renner, Daniel Cho, Jennifer Chuong, and Nerijus Petrokas. We are also grateful to the numerous students and interns who have shared their energy and enthusiasm: Jimmy Shen, Saran Oki, Yusun Kwon, Liz Burrow, James Smith, Dan Smithwick, Joseph Michael, Buck Sleeper, Ryan Murphy, James Graham, Ryan Pinkham, Lisa Pauli, Teddy Huyck, Brian Yang, Orlin Zhekov, Daniel Yi-Hsiang Chao, Kate Cho, James Forren, Minsoo Lee, Angie Müller, Gabriel Cira, Lizzie Krasner, Shani Cho, Kyle Steinfeld, Marlene Kuhn, Naomi Munro, Tim Morsehead, Alex Miller, Stylianos Dristas, Amy Yang, Eddie Can, Saeed Arida, Becca Edson, Sawako Kaijima, Shuji Suzumori, Cathy Kim, Milena Tsvetkova, Jon Braddock, Bren Galvez-Moretti, and Pete DePasquale. Our collaborators deserve special thanks for productive interactions and ongoing dialogue: Matthew Reynolds, Will Pickering, Paul Kassabian, Erik Carlson, and Franco Vairani.

We also acknowledge the support from clients and sponsors: Abby Stillman, Sam and Leslie Davol, Tony Pangaro, Kathy MacNeil, Sam and Song Chung, Hilary Thomas, Jill Kaplan, Mark Green, Mike Keltz, Joseph Hsu, Doug Rivera, Anastasia Hulsizer, Jeremy Liu, Michael Höweler, and Kim Dupcak. We have benefited from the support of individuals and institutions: Rosalie Genevro and Anne Reiselbach at the Architectural League, Pamela Puchalski and Rick Bell at the Center for Architecture, Richard Fitzgerald at the Boston Society of Architects, and Sarah Herda at the Graham Foundation for Advanced Studies in the Fine Arts.

We would like to acknowledge our mentors in the firms we were fortunate enough to be a part of during our formative years as architects: Kathryn Dean and Chuck Wolf (Dean Wolf Architects), Bill Pedersen and Paul Katz (Kohn Pedersen Fox), and Liz Diller, Ric Scofidio, and Charles Renfro (Diller Scofidio + Renfro).

We are grateful to the guidance and inspiration of colleagues and mentors from various institutions where we have taught: at MIT, Adele Naude-Santos, Nader Tehrani, Yungho Chang, Andrew Scott, Mark Jarzombek, Stanford Anderson, Ann Pendelton-Jullian, Sheila Kennedy, Ana Miljacki, Mark Goulthorpe, Arindam Dutta, Alexander D'Hooghe, John Ochsendorf, and John Fernandez; at Harvard GSD, Mohsen Mostafavi, Toshiko Mori, Scott Cohen, Laura Miller, Mariana Ibañez, Lluis Ortega, and Andrea Leers; at the University of Toronto, John Shnier, Bridgette Shim, Ante Liu, Shayne Williamson, Betsy Williamson, and Peter Yeadon; and at the City College of New York, Andrew Zago.

We would like to thank our colleagues and friends for their support, inspiration, and camaraderie: Karel Klein, Hayley Eber, Frank Gesualdi, Josh Uhl, Flavio Stigliano, Gaspar Libedinsky, Gerri Davis, Michael Arad, David Lewis, Marc Tsurumaki, Paul Lewis, Eric Bunge, Mimi Hoang, Marcelo Spina, Lisa Iwamoto, Ashley Schafer, Amanda Reeser Lawrence, Ben Gilmartin, Irina Verona, Don Schillingberg, Thomas Demonchaux, Michael Meredith, John Hong, Jin Hee Park, Beth Whittaker, Mark Pasnik, Hansy Better, Anthony Piermarini, Tim Love, Tiffany Lin, Mark Oldham, Shauna Gillies-Smith, Axel Killian, Kazys Varnelis, Mimi Zeiger, Olga Bakic, and Rose Mendez.

Much of the work in this publication would not have been possible without the generous support of the Fulbright Association, the Massachusetts Institute of Technology, the MIT Council for the Arts, the Athena Award from the Rhode Island School of Design, Printed Matter, the Whitney Museum of American Art, the Graham Foundation for Advanced Studies in the Fine Arts, and the American Academy in Rome.

Special thanks to Kevin Lippert and Jennifer Thompson from Princeton Architectural Press. In the dialogue leading to the formulation of the book and the essays that are included here, we thank the authors for their feedback and critical comments: Rodolphe el-Khoury, Andrew Payne, Filip Tejchman, and Brooke Hodge. We would like to thank Alice Chung at Omnivore for the book's graphic design.

Lastly, we'd like to thank our parents for their love and support: Hannah Yoon, Jason Yoon, Ichun Jane Höweler, and Reinhardt Höweler.